NUTRITION MATTERS

It took us 25 years to get to the point that better nutrition is accepted in development circles as being important and there is a willingness to do something major about it. This is no longer a pipe dream. Is it going to take another 25 years for us to make this happen? Knowing what we know, to continue business as usual would be the ultimate case of *nutrition malpractice* — of which we all would be guilty (*Berg, 1991*).

For Jos and George

NUTRITION MATTERS

People Food and Famine

HELEN YOUNG and SUSANNE JASPARS

INTERMEDIATE TECHNOLOGY PUBLICATIONS 1995

Intermediate Technology Publications Ltd,
103–105 Southampton Row, London WC1B 4HH, UK.

A CIP catalogue record for this book
is available from the British Library

ISBN 1 85339 243 X

Typeset by Dorwyn Ltd, Rowlands Castle, Hants
Printed in Great Britain by BPC Wheatons Ltd, Exeter

CONTENTS

Figures

Tables

ACKNOWLEDGEMENTS

Many people have helped us with this book, including those who worked with us in Darfur and elsewhere, and those who supported our research in the UK. The research and preparations for this book were supported by grants from the Health and Population Division, ODA, the Economic and Social Council for Research, ODA, and Oxfam. The Health and Population Division also generously provided a book subsidy.

The Food Security Unit at the Institute of Development Studies, University of Sussex, were especially important as they enabled us to join them for a year as Visiting Research Fellows, which provided us with a stimulating environment and practical support. Simon Maxwell, Margie Buchanan-Smith and Susanna Davies gave useful comments on earlier drafts.

Others who deserve credit are those people in Darfur working for Oxfam and also local volunteers, including Peter Strachan, Bedreldin Shutta, Karin de Jonge, Radiya Abukkar, Shadiya Mohamed, Abdulgadir Omar, Asadiq Amir and Haneina in El Fasher; Medina Fadlasid, Musa Ahmed, Nafisa Abukkar, and Omar Abukkar in Malha; also Yusif Abukkar, Musa Abukkar, Halima Bakheet, Sa'adiya Ahmed in Mareiga; and finally Umsalama Mohammed, Roqiya Sayim, Abdullayahya Khatir, Su'aad Juma, and Mohammed Abdulrahim in Cuma.

Many people who worked for other agencies in Darfur also helped and supported us; Simon Mollison, Seif Eldein, Taj Eldein, Mohammed Ahmed from Save the Children Fund; Dr Abdulgabar Fadul, Margie Buchanan-Smith, Kay Sharp, Alex Lincoln, David Hybert from the Agricultural Planning Unit; and Simon Croxton and Mohammed Siddiq from the Intermediate Technology Development Group.

Our influences are many, including all those who attended the workshop on 'Nutritional Surveillance; Help or Hindrance in Times of Famine' and those who commented on the workshop discussion paper. In particular for detailed comments we would like to thank Judith Appleton, Marleen Boelaart, Andre Briend, Robert Chambers, Urban Jonsson, Nigel Padfield, Phillip Payne, John Seaman, Alex de Waal, and Ken Wilson. We also thank those who participated in discussions on our work at the Liverpool School of Tropical Medicine, the London School of Hygiene and Tropical Medicine, and the Institute of Social Studies in the Hague.

Thanks to Mike, Sarah and George at System Simulation who enabled us to keep in touch between Nairobi and London as the final version of this book was completed. In Nairobi we thank the various members of the UNHCR 'radio room'.

Finally thank you to those close friends and family whose support made us persevere: Bea Jaspars, Robert Blackburn, Jeannie Chamberlain and Sue Chowdhury.

ABBREVIATIONS

ACC/SCN	Administrative Committee on Coordination/ Sub Committee on Nutrition
APU	Agricultural Planning Unit (Darfur, Sudan)
CDC	Centers for Disease Control, Atlanta, Georgia, USA
EC	European Community
EPI	Expanded Programme of Immunization
EWS	Early Warning System(s)
FAO	Food and Agriculture Organization
HFA	Height-for-Age
LS	Sudanese pounds
LRCS	League of Red Cross Societies (now International Federation of Red Cross Societies — IFRCS)
MSF	Médecins Sans Frontières
MUAC	Mid Upper Arm Circumference
MOH	Ministry of Health
NCHS	National Center for Health Statistics, USA
NGO	Non Governmental Organization
ODA	Overseas Development Administration
PEM	Protein Energy Malnutrition
PRA	Participatory Rural Appraisal
RAP	Rapid Assessment Procedure
RRA	Rapid Rural Appraisal
RRC	Relief and Rehabilitation Commission
SCF	Save the Children Fund, UK
SD	Standard Deviation
SERISS	Sudan Emergency and Recovery Information and Surveillance System
SRC	Sudanese Red Crescent
USAID	United States Agency for International Development
UNICEF	United Nations Children's Fund
WFA	Weight-for-Age
WFH	Weight-for-Height
WFP	World Food Programme
WHO	World Health Organization
WRO	Western Relief Operation

INTRODUCTION

The context of famine relief and refugee crises has changed dramatically over the past 15 years. Problems of inadequate nutrition are escalating, especially in Africa, where unprecedented numbers of displaced people and refugees are now dependent on international relief. Numbers of official refugees increased from 1.5 million in 1951, to some 18 million in 1992 (UNHCR, 1994). To these numbers must be added an estimated 20 million displaced people who do not fall under the refugee category (UNHCR, 1994). These figures can significantly increase in days; in one week alone in 1991 1.5 million refugees flooded the border areas of Iraq, Turkey and Iran. Within three weeks of the deaths of the presidents of Rwanda and Burundi on 6 April 1994, 0.9 million refugees fled ethnic violence to neighbouring countries, leaving behind many thousands displaced (UNHCR, 1994).

No doubt, the worst humanitarian disasters are now likely to be a result of civil conflict and war, where even the lives of aid workers are under threat. The world's attention is focused on the effects of the very worst emergencies, and with some justification, as massive population displacements call for urgent action to provide the basic essentials of life. These acute emergencies overshadow the less severe famines and long-term protracted emergencies, which often go unnoticed by the media, even though in numbers and in financial terms they exceed the acute emergencies. The response to these situations is usually limited to more of the same relief measures that are adopted during an acute emergency, which are often inappropriate given the opportunities to support or rebuild people's livelihoods.

Nutrition matters in all situations of food insecurity and famine, because issues of food and nutrition are central, whether it is a matter of immediate survival or longer-term recovery and development. Yet if we expect to get the action right and make an impact on malnutrition and food insecurity, we need to know how and why nutrition matters, not just from the point of view as outsiders, but also from the perspective of insiders. This is why we have written this book.

We have combined our practical insights as fieldworkers with the wider body of knowledge about nutrition and famine. We found that the role of nutrition in relation to famine as described in the available literature was either unclear or over-simplified, which partly explains why the recommended approaches to nutrition often seem inadequate or at least misplaced. Recent practical experience can now point the way ahead and help find solutions to today's nutritional problems.

As nutritionists working for agencies like Oxfam, Médecins Sans Frontières and UNHCR, we have been involved in nutritional assessments and surveys in sub-Saharan Africa, Asia and Latin America. Between 1988 and 1990 we both worked in Darfur, Sudan, and strived to set up a nutritional surveillance system more in keeping with the needs of local people, while still responding to the information needs of national decision makers. In some ways we turned our backs on conventional wisdom, and based our approach on the actual experience of nutritional assessments in sub-Saharan Africa during the seventies and eighties.

Often during our previous work in Africa we had proved unable to apply correctly the standard procedures. Asked to carry out assessments and surveys by international agencies, we willingly went off, armed with tape-measures, scales and 'weight-for-height' charts, expecting to find out at least how many were malnourished, and, hopefully, who they were, where and why.

Not surprisingly, it was never that easy. Almost immediately we would be thwarted in our good intentions – usually by time constraints, but more often by the impracticality of doing surveys in such difficult circumstances. Darfur is a good case in point: it is half the size of Kenya, has a widely scattered population of unknown size, and the lack of roads and constant fuel shortages make travel extremely difficult. This is not to mention the turmoil and confusion that accompanies an international relief operation.

Not only was it difficult to apply the standard survey methods but also it often seemed inappropriate. Nutritionists usually find themselves working in isolation from their professional colleagues, but during the few opportunities we had to meet it was apparent that we faced common problems. Many nutritionists have to modify and adapt the conventional approach to surveys, yet this is rarely if ever reported because of the danger of casting doubt on survey results.

Despite the increasing experience of nutrition in emergencies, the conventional nutritional wisdom applied today is still by and large derived from purely technical considerations, rather than practical experience. Nutritionists have been slow to adopt a more people-centred approach in their work. Nutritional surveillance is still usually a centrally conceived idea with little regard for local people's perceptions or felt needs.

We want to bring to light the practical difficulties faced by fieldworkers, and show how we developed an alternative approach to nutritional assessments and surveillance in Darfur. The approach we took in Darfur is by no means applicable in every situation, but by demystifying and explaining the basis of assessment procedures and techniques, we hope to enable readers to decide the best approach in their situation.

Structure and content

The book is divided into three parts and seven chapters. Part 1 is a review of contemporary views of famine and nutrition, including concepts of nutrition and famine (Chapter 1); nutritional surveillance for famine early warning (Chapter 2); and methods for assessments and surveillance (Chapter 3).

Part 2 reveals nutrition in action, and presents a detailed case-study of nutritional surveillance in Darfur, Sudan, 1984 to 1991, including the development of a new community-based approach to surveillance from 1988.

Part 3 looks to the future and brings together past experience and knowledge to generate a conceptual framework for understanding the role of nutrition in famine. This helps analyse who is affected by famine, how, when and why and is linked to practical issues of assessment, interventions and targeting. Finally obstacles to a more effective role for nutrition in emergencies are discussed.

For most people, famine is about hunger, starvation and death. Malnutrition is often the focus of the popularized images of famine presented by the media. This idea that malnutrition is a final outcome of famine linked with death is very limited. It assumes that as long as people are able to obtain food, they will do so in order to avoid starvation and death. People's actual response to famine contradicts this assumption; they often choose to go hungry in order to preserve their meagre resources. Concepts of famine and malnutrition are reviewed in Chapter 1.

Nutritional surveillance is often part of famine early warning systems, which aim to predict and so prevent famines. Standard uses of nutritional data in early warning systems, reflect the limited view of malnutrition as an outcome of famine, rather than a predictor. It is used to advocate food aid, and to decide who should receive it. But in practice, high rates of acute malnutrition may be evident long before the height of the famine, as we often found in Darfur. Furthermore, malnutrition at this stage may not be accompanied by famine deaths.

This understanding led us to develop a new conceptual framework for understanding nutrition in relation to famine, which is presented in Chapter 1 and developed further in Chapter 6. The point of this framework is to try and make sense of the events that occur prior to and during famine, including coping strategies and malnutrition. The framework should enable better interpretation of nutritional information and so help identify more appropriate interventions, and targeting strategies.

To mount international appeals and justify the need for food aid, the focus of nutrition surveys has been on outcomes – nutritional statistics, such as the prevalence rates of malnutrition. Much less attention is given to understanding causes. For the purposes of advocacy, the apparent objectivity of nutritional data is invaluable. The reliability and validity of data are rarely questioned, as long as the standard methods of data collection are used. In 1988, our doubts about the validity of large-scale surveys prompted us to undertake smaller more manageable assessments of individual communities that took account not only of outcomes, but also underlying causes and the processes leading to a decline in food security. The willing co-operation of people from the communities was vital from the beginning of the programme. As it proceded it became apparent that not only their co-operation but also their active participation was necessary, to such a degree that the continuation of the programme was dependent on them alone. In the long run any project or programme fails unless local people feel they benefit from it and want to sustain it. This was the greatest challenge facing us, and over the years in Darfur, we worked to establish a community-based nutritional surveillance programme in which the locus of power was shared more fairly between the local people and outsiders.

This approach met with some small success. In 1990, it survived the turbulent political changes that prompted donors to withdraw funding of development programmes in Sudan and led to the collapse of the Darfur early warning system. The only remaining component of the system was the community-based nutritional surveillance, which continued to provide data and information.

In the past decade alone Darfur has experienced three separate international relief programmes, which have cost donors millions of dollars. Yet these 'band aids' have failed either to halt long-term economic decline, or to promote the development of the region: success in either would have reduced the impact of drought on food security. As history continues to repeat itself we should take heed of even the smallest achievements and build upon them, rather than reverting to temporary relief measures that are part of the vicious circle of food insecurity and famine spiralling downwards into greater decline and dependency.

Note on terminology

We have decided to use the popular terms of convenience, malnutrition and nutritional status in place of the more physiologically correct terms: growth failure and anthropometric status. Although growth failure and malnutrition are by no means the same thing, the popular terms are in common use in practical situations of food insecurity and famine.

PART 1
NUTRITION AND FAMINE
Contemporary Views and Practice

CHAPTER 1

Understanding famine and malnutrition

Famines are by no means a thing of the past; new emergencies are regularly reported by the media and the stream of refugees and people affected by famine increases daily. In many parts of Africa, the occasional fluctuations in food supply have been exaggerated into a continuous cycle of food scarcity and famine. In the last decade, some parts of Africa have experienced protracted emergencies drawn out over several years. Others, such as Darfur, have experienced recurrent episodes of drought and food insecurity which have prompted many separate international emergency relief operations.

For most of us the word famine conjures up images of starving people, huddled by the roadside or crowded into makeshift camps. Malnourished children immediately spring to mind, nursed by mothers unable to feed them. These images appear almost daily on the TV or in newspapers, so much so that we expect to see children on the verge of dying from malnutrition before we think of it as a serious famine. These pictures depict people with a look of helpless resignation, all because of an apparent lack of food. Yet just how realistic are these impressions of famine?

This chapter gives an overview of current ideas of famine, and of the principles of nutrition which are relevant to famine and food security. The relationship between nutrition and disease is essential to an understanding of famine. The links between nutrition and famine seem obvious but as this chapter unfolds, you will see that starvation may just as well be a means of survival as it is a cause of death.

Current views on famine

Lack of food, hunger, starvation and eventually death are all accepted as part of 'famine', yet in most cases famine is not just a simple matter of lack of food leading to starvation and death. Views of famine have evolved from a definition based on this simple causal relationship to a broader understanding of why famine happens and what causes famine deaths.

Starvation means that communities, families and individuals are unable to obtain enough food for their needs, which in peacetime does not happen overnight. In peacetime, famine is usually a slow process, gradually worsening until finally starvation and death can no longer be avoided. In less severe famines, there may be no excess deaths at all, instead acute poverty may slowly deplete people's resources and their ability to cope, but may not immediately endanger their lives.

Traditionally, we think of famine as precipitated by drought, but recent emergencies have highlighted the multi-causality of famines and the increasing role of war and conflict in creating famine. Peacetime famines are by comparison usually much less severe than war-related famines. War creates famine in different ways, which are explored by de Waal (1993), and briefly described in Box 1.1. In these ways the very tactics of war create famine, and so inevitably humanitarian aid becomes caught up in the dynamics of conflict, and become part of the war economy (Pallister, 1994).

Box 1.1   How war creates famine in Africa

o Armies requisition grain and other foods, including international food aid.
o At a national level, military budgets consume vast amounts of resources that would otherwise be available for services or development.
o The destruction by armies of houses, crops, food stores, livestock, infrastructure (transport networks, dams, clinics, schools) and damage to the environment.
o Large areas of land are lost to mines and military infrastructure, such as trenches and encampments.
o War and violence prevent people from following the strategies that would otherwise allow them to cope with a disaster. They may be restricted to 'protected' villages, or living under siege.
o Control of trade may contribute to localized famines.
o Social disintegration means that people no longer have the social and kinship links that help them survive a period of drought.

Apart from the direct effects of war and violence, in parts of Africa there has been a long-term political process of discrimination and ostracism, as particular ethnic groups have been oppressed for specific reasons (Duffield, 1994). For example, oppression of the Rahanweyn, in Somalia (de Waal, 1993) and of the Dinka of Bahr el Ghazal, in southern Sudan (Keen, 1991). Other factors contributing to complex emergencies include the failure of development, and the long-term decline and fragmentation of formal economies and social structures (Duffield, 1994).

Entitlement theory

Until Amartya Sen (1981) proposed his entitlement theory to explain the cause of famine, it was widely believed that famine was the result of a decline in the availability of food caused by a failure in food production from natural causes. Sen showed that famine and starvation are not solely related to overall food supplies, but are the result of a decline in people's access to food or, as he termed it, a decline in their 'exchange entitlements'.

4

In Sen's words famine and starvation are the result of:

some people not *having* enough food to eat, not the characteristic of there not *being enough food to eat'.*

Sen identified four different types of exchange entitlements; through trade, own production, own labour, inheritance or other type of asset transfer. Famine occurs when a large number of people have reached a stage when their exchange entitlements have failed to meet their minimum food needs and those of their families.

Exchange entitlements fluctuate according to the changing nature of people's sources of livelihood and the prevailing market conditions. For example, local employment opportunities and wage rates influence income from waged labour. Local market prices influence income from sale of produce or capital assets and also the cost of essential purchases, such as food. Consequently, exchange entitlements can worsen as a result of a variety of events, for example, a failure in demand caused by unemployment or a devaluation of people's assets caused by inflation, or a decline in food supply leading to food shortages and inflation.

Box 1.2   Examples of failures in exchange entitlements

The Bengal famine in 1943
Food availability was not much lower than in the preceding five years. Exchange entitlements of agricultural labourers were drastically reduced because the escalating cost of rice was not matched by an increase in their wage rates. The price of rice was forced up by the combined effects of war, hoarding and speculation, and rice export restrictions in other provinces, rather than a decline in food production.

The Ethiopian famine of 1972–1974
The exchange entitlements of pastoralists are largely based on the sale of livestock to buy grain. As a result of the drought and subsequent high grain prices, pastoralists were forced to sell more animals than normal. A fall in livestock prices led to a dramatic decline in their grain–livestock exchange entitlement. In other words they needed to sell increasing numbers of livestock in order to buy sufficient grain for their needs.

From 'Poverty and Famines, An Essay on Entitlement and Deprivation', by Amartya Sen, 1981, Clarendon Press, Oxford.

The concept of entitlements applies to countries as well as to individuals. It is not necessarily countries that suffer a reduction in food production that experience famine. During 1980–85 and 1975–85, sub-Sahelian countries which did not have famine had a greater decline in food production per head than other countries that did experience famine. In those countries that did experience famine, the decline in food production had not been compensated for by an expansion of alternative incomes and imports (Dreze and Sen, 1989).

Entitlement theory has advanced our understanding of famine by providing a framework for analysing the underlying causes of famines. This has been extended and developed by other famine analysts. Swift (1989) describes three proximate causes of famine, one of which is 'entitlements', defined by him more narrowly as 'exchange relationships'. The other two proximate causes of famine are a failure in production, and a failure in household access to assets (investments, stores and legitimate claims on help from other people or organizations including government). All other causes, such as drought, war and the like, produce an effect through their influence on these three proximate causes. In common with many recent famine researchers he emphasizes the importance of analysing the responses households or communities make to vulnerability and famine threat.

Local views of famine

Different views of famine
People affected by drought and famine view it differently from those who only witness its disastrous final effects. They distinguish between the different types of famine according to their severity. Turkana herders in Kenya and the people of Darfur, Sudan, distinguish between famines that kill and those that do not kill (de Waal, 1989a; Swift, 1989). In Darfur, the names of more severe famines often imply hunger, destitution or social breakdown, whereas those for less severe famines may refer to shortage of grain, places where people obtained food, or to wild foods eaten (de Waal, 1989a). In Bangladesh, three types of famine are recognized; scarcity, when times are bad; famine, when alms are scarce; and nation-wide famine, when the epoch changes (Currey, 1978). The Massa and Mussey of Chad and Cameroon also distinguish between various levels of food shortage, ranging from 'mayra', hunger, to 'baknarda', starvation. Only 'baknarda' is associated with people dying (de Garine and Kappert, 1988).

Focus on famine deaths or social breakdown
People who have experienced famine emphasize the economic disruption, social breakdown and destitution that is part of famine. This contrasts with the view of outsiders who tend to focus on the outcome of famine— starvation and famine deaths. Long before famine deaths occur people are aware of the threat of famine building up, and for them famine is a long process. In many African famines people have identified the beginning of their problems several years before the distress migration and famine deaths.

Coping strategies

People facing regular episodes of drought and famine have developed complex strategies for coping with these events. The main aim of 'coping

6

strategies' is to preserve productive assets which are needed to sustain a living in the future. For farmers, these assets might be their draught animals, farm tools, land, or cash to pay for essential farm inputs.

Coping strategies vary according to livelihoods, systems of land use, marketing and credit. People learn through experience of drought and famine which specific strategies are best in their situation. Even though local circumstances differ, researchers have found that coping strategies tend to follow a similar pattern.

Corbett (1988) divides this sequence into three stages: the first stage is the adoption of 'insurance strategies' which are carefully planned in anticipation of environmental uncertainty and seasonal food shortages. The strategies in the next two stages are crisis responses brought about by repeated crop failure or prolonged disruption of production and marketing because of, for example, war. Strategies employed during the second stage threaten the households' future productive capacity, while in the third and final stage households become destitute and the only response left is to migrate. The severity of famine can often be distinguished by the strategies that people adopt.

Insurance strategies are intended to minimize the risks of production and to manage shortfalls in production (Frankenberger and Goldstein, 1990). As the season unfolds and drought appears increasingly likely, farmers try to minimize their risks of production by altering cropping patterns. Similarly, livestock owners restructure herds in favour of drought-resistant animals.

In anticipation of shortfalls in crop production, farmers may have a number of options: they build up stores of food or assets in good years, they develop social networks which can be called upon in lean times, and they diversify their sources of income to include off-farm income. Having several diverse sources of income reduces the risks. If any one source fails to give a return, there is some security provided as long as they do not all fail at the same time. Possessions which are not needed for production can be sold without endangering the future livelihood of the household.

People often consciously make changes to their diet in response to food shortages related to drought. This may involve a switch to cheaper, less desirable and perhaps less nutritious foods, or a reduction in the number or size of meals eaten. Examples of dietary change as an early response to insecurity are given in Box 2.2, Chapter 2, page 37.

In many parts of Africa, the collection and consumption of wild foods is a common strategy during periods of food insecurity; these might include plants, roots and berries. Wild foods are a normal part of the diet for some groups, although their consumption may increase during periods of food insecurity. There are other wild foods that are only consumed during times of stress which are usually entirely different species from those collected in normal times. The use of wild foods in Darfur, Sudan, is described in the case-study in Chapter 4 (page 66).

Insurance strategies involve only a small commitment of domestic resources and are readily reversible once the situation has improved. People employ insurance strategies for as long as possible to postpone the sale of essential assets. The short-term cost of going hungry is preferable to long-term impoverishment and the threat of destitution.

The transition from insurance to crisis strategies occurs when the available insurance strategies are no longer adequate. This happens when many people adopt the same strategies at the same time—for example, large numbers of people seeking work depresses wages, or widespread livestock sales lead to a collapse in market prices. Sometimes people are prevented from following their normal insurance strategies because of civil conflict or war. This speeding up of events often precipitates the most severe famines.

New strategies have to be found when these initial responses prove inadequate and the crisis continues. Later strategies threaten the economic welfare of the household as assets are depleted and debts build up. It becomes increasingly unlikely that members of the household will be able to resort to their former livelihoods once the crisis is over.

Eventually the destitute are driven from their homes in a desperate search for charity or other means of survival.[1] The distress migration of whole households usually represents the last phase of famine, which is in contrast to the earlier migration of individual family members who left

---

Table 1.1 Examples of responses to household food shortage

Insurance strategies
o Changes in cropping patterns
o Restructuring herds in favour of more drought-resistant animals
o Sale of non-productive assets
o Drawing on stores and assets
o Loans—drawing on social/business networks
o Labour migration
o Sale of small livestock
o Collection of wild foods
o Reduction of food intake
o Changes in dietary patterns

Crisis strategies
o Sale of productive assets
o Mortgaging farmland
o Sale of farmland
o Distress migration

---

[1] People may be forced to leave their homes because of a lack of water as a result of drought, rather than a lack of food.

8

home to look for temporary work elsewhere. In those areas that experienced drought and drought relief in the mid-seventies and early eighties, petitioning the local authorities for assistance has become one of their coping strategies, but is usually tried as soon as crops fail rather than as a later strategy (Kelly, 1992; de Waal, 1989a).

Loss of livelihood and destitution cause severe social disruption. Distress migration often leads to the creation of famine camps, where people congregate in the hope of receiving assistance. Once conditions improve, people usually return home if there is a chance of rebuilding what they have lost.

Often those who suffer most during drought are those who are least able to diversify their sources of income in normal times because they possess few assets and have limited access to land, credit and other resources. They may not have recovered from previous episodes of drought and famine and are considerably impoverished as a result. External risks and shocks, such as drought, war or conflict, affect households to different degrees; some suffer temporary hardships, others are brought to the brink of destitution, while some profit from the situation.

Vulnerability is not necessarily the same as poverty. It implies an inability to cope or to deal with the consequences of drought, civil conflict or other risks and shocks. Although many poor people are vulnerable, they are not necessarily so, as they may have greater defences against external shocks than those households which have considerable assets. Political vulnerability is especially important in complex emergencies, as entire social or ethnic groups may be subjected to discrimination and intimidation, or even violence and human rights abuse, depending on circumstances (Duffield, 1994).

A guided tour of malnutrition

To understand undernutrition in relation to famine, it is important to consider the underlying causes of malnutrition, and the associated risks of disease and death. The clinical condition of protein energy malnutrition is described fully by Waterlow (1992).

Defining malnutrition

Malnutrition includes a wide range of clinical disorders that are the result of an inadequate intake of energy and protein, as well as other nutrients. The growth of young children, pregnancy, lactation and physical work are all impaired.

The terms malnutrition and undernutrition are often used interchangeably, which is confusing. For our purposes, we consider undernutrition to refer to a reduced food intake in relation to a recommended dietary intake.

9

Box 1.3   Stunting and wasting

Wasting reflects recent rapid weight loss or a failure to gain weight. Wasting is readily reversible once conditions improve. Wasting is evidence of acute PEM.

Stunting reflects a height deficit which develops over a long period of time as a result of prolonged poor nutrition. Unlike wasting the development of stunting is a slow, cumulative process and it may not be evident for some years, at which time nutrition may have improved. By two years of age, height deficits may be irreversible. Stunting is evidence of chronic PEM.

We are mostly concerned with protein energy malnutrition (PEM). The two extreme forms of PEM are marasmus and kwashiorkor. Milder forms of PEM are much more widespread. PEM among children is characterized by growth failure, wasting (thinness) or stunting (shortness), or a combination of both.

Measuring malnutrition

The two types of growth failure, wasting and stunting, are measured by taking the weight and height measurements of children, and converting these into nutritional indices, such as weight-for-height, height-for-age and weight-for-age.[2] The measurements of an individual are compared with reference values and transformed into their nutritional status. For example, to assess weight-for-height, a child's weight is compared with the weight of the reference child of the same height.

Since 1978, the WHO has recommended the use of an international growth reference based on samples of American children from the US National Center for Health Statistics (Dibley *et al.*, 1987). This allows comparisons between countries.

For assessments of recent nutrition the weight-for-height nutritional index is appropriate because it reflects short-term growth failure or acute malnutrition related to weight loss (wasting). Weight-for-height is the recommended nutritional index for assessment of short-term nutritional problems and for monitoring nutritional status for early warning systems (Beaton *et al.*, 1990). A major advantage of weight-for-height for field surveys is that it is unnecessary to determine the age of the child, unlike the height-for-age or weight-for-age indices. During one-off surveys, age is difficult and time consuming to assess accurately.

---

[2] Mid-upper arm circumference (MUAC) is also used to assess wasting. It changes little between one and five years of age and so is considered independent of age.

Box 1.4   Widely used nutritional indices

Weight-for-height   Reflects recent weight loss or gain, and is the best indicator of wasting. Useful when age is unknown. Recommended for assessments of recent nutrition and useful for assessments of famine and refugee situations.

Height-for-age   Reflects skeletal growth, and is the best indicator of stunting. The longer time scale over which height-for-age is affected makes it more useful for long-term planning and policy development rather than emergencies (Beaton *et al.*, 1990).

Weight-for-age   A composite index, which reflects either wasting or stunting or a combination of both. Rapidly changing weight-for-age can be assumed to be the result of changing weight-for-height, while low weight-for-age among older children may be a result of low height-for-age. Growth charts based on weight-for-age reference curves are used for growth monitoring in mother and child health clinics.

Anthropometry as an indicator of malnutrition

A child's anthropometric status is related to a reference population, and described either by the standard deviation score (SD score) or the percentage of the reference median.[3]

The SD score uses the frequency distribution of the reference population and is a measure of the distance between the child's measurement and the median of the reference population. This is expressed in multiples of the standard deviation of the distribution curve for the reference population (Figure 1.1). SD scores are also termed 'Z scores'.

The percentage of the median expresses a child's measurement as a percentage of the median (mean) of the reference population.

For each nutritional index there are 'cut-off points' which are used to categorize malnutrition. These are statistically determined based on the distribution curve of the reference population. A child whose measurement falls below −2 SDs weight-for-height is classified as moderately malnourished, while an SD score below −3 is classified as severely malnourished.

A weight-for-height SD score of −2 roughly corresponds to 80 per cent of the median, and a weight-for-height SD score of −3 roughly corresponds to 70 per cent of the median.

---

[3] Body Mass Index is an indicator of the nutritional status of adults and is calculated by dividing weight by height squared. Average BMI in most adult groups in less-developed countries is in the range from 19 to 21 (James *et al.*, 1988).

11

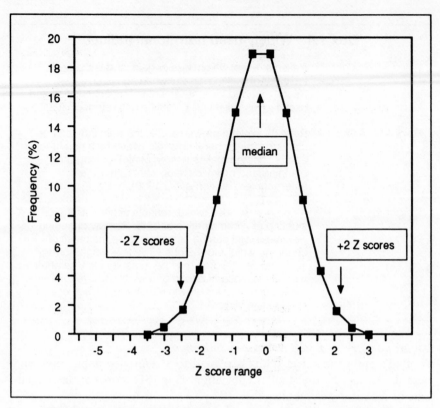

Figure 1.1   The distribution curve of the reference population

Nutritional indices are also used to assess the nutritional status of populations. Population assessments are usually based on the nutritional status of a representative sample of children under five years of age. Results are presented as the prevalence of children who fall below the cut-off point (–2 SD scores or 80 per cent WFH), or as the mean SD score or mean percentage of the nutrition index. In theory, more than 2.5 per cent of children below –2 Z scores (<80 per cent) can be viewed as abnormal. In practice this varies seasonally with no obvious harmful effects.

Causes of malnutrition

Malnutrition can have many causes. The two immediate causes of malnutrition in an individual are an inadequate diet and infectious disease, and they frequently occur together. These in turn are determined by numerous underlying causes.

In the past, malnutrition was thought to be a medical problem with a single cause: protein deficiency. The 'protein gap' as it was known, was thought to be the most widespread nutritional problem and was cured by

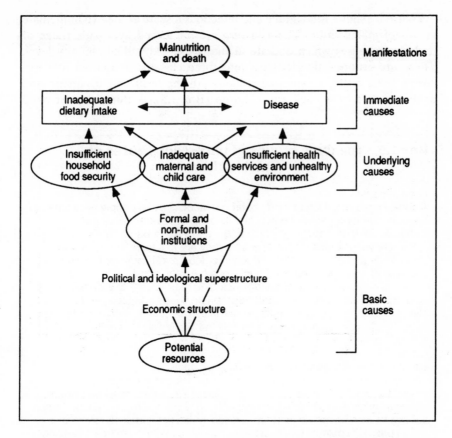

Figure 1.2 A conceptual framework showing the causes of malnutrition
(UNICEF, 1990)

high-protein foods. By the mid-seventies, energy intake became a key issue
as the interaction between protein and energy was recognized. This raised
social and economic issues of access to food by the poor, and malnutrition
was no longer only a medical problem to be treated. Poverty and the
conditions associated with it are now recognized as the overriding causes of
malnutrition.

The underlying causes of malnutrition can be described with the help of
a model which shows the various factors and how they are interlinked.
Figure 1.2 shows the conceptual framework proposed by UNICEF (1990),
which is relatively simple and can be adapted to develop locally specific
models of malnutrition. The framework distinguishes between causes
which operate at different levels of society, starting with the household,
and working backwards to include the community, district or region and
country. This is helpful as particular problems must be addressed at the
appropriate level.

13

Figure 1.2 shows food intake and infectious disease as the two immediate causes of malnutrition. These in turn are influenced by a wide range of underlying causes which operate at the household and community level. These are grouped by UNICEF into three clusters: household food security, basic health services combined with the health environment, and adequate care of women and children (Box 1.5). A third level of basic

---

Box 1.5 The three groups of underlying causes of malnutrition

Food security
A widely used definition of food security is 'access by all people at all times to enough food for an active healthy life. Its essential elements are the availability of food and the ability to acquire it'. (World Bank, 1986).

For a household this means how able they are to secure adequate food, either through their own food production or food purchases, for meeting the needs of all their members. The ability of a household to produce food depends on a wide range of factors including their access to available fertile land, the availability of labour and appropriate seeds and tools, and the climatic conditions. Food purchases are influenced on the one hand by the household's income, and on the other by the availability and prices of foods in local markets.

Basic health services and the health environment
The health environment influences exposure to infectious disease. Environmental factors that increase exposure to disease include: limited water supply, poor sanitation, a crowded household with many young children, contaminated surface water, unhygienic food preparation, and a hot and dusty dry season.

The provision of local health services, and access to those health services, influence treatment of infection. Inadequate or late treatment places a child at increased nutritional risk by prolonging the disease. Local health services are often understaffed or have a limited supply of essential drugs. Alternatively, health-care services may be well developed but prohibitively expensive and therefore unavailable to the poor. Attitudes to health care affect willingness to make use of the services.

Maternal and child care
Child care and sound feeding practices are needed for good nutrition and health. The care of the child is affected by a wide range of behaviours that in turn affect child nutrition. There is the direct care of the child by members of the family, in particular the mother. But of equal importance are other behaviours that indirectly affect care of the child, for example, the support given by the family or community to the adult members of the family, and the behaviours that influence how the household food supply is shared among its members, or attitudes to modern health services, water supplies and sanitation.

Often the care of children is closely linked with the situation of women. If the status of women is low they may have little control over the resources within the family; so although they may have major responsibilities for childrearing they do not have the resources to carry it out.

14

causes is influenced by potential resources, economic structure, and the political and ideological superstructure.

In practice the three groups of underlying causes interact with one another. In particular, the care of children is heavily infuenced by the food security of the household and access to health services. For example, if a mother is having to spend long hours doing agricultural work in fields far from her home to provide the family's food, she will have relatively less time to select and prepare nutritious meals and to respond to the emotional needs of her children.

Box 1.6   Interaction between measles, diarrhoea and growth status

Effect of measles and diarrhoea on growth status
Fever increases energy expenditure by 10–15 per cent for each 1°C rise in body temperature. Measles profoundly affects appetite, and may reduce food intake for several weeks following infection. Either of these two factors can lead to dramatic weight loss and wasting.

Measles occurring in poor environments is associated with growth faltering, vitamin-A deficiency and immune suppression. The immune suppression can persist for up to four months after infection, which partly explains the particular risk of respiratory and diarrhoeal complications of measles and the relatively greater severity of the disease in poor communities. Measles and diarrhoea appear to act synergistically; greater growth deficits are found in children among whom measles is complicated by diarrhoea.

Repeated attacks of diarrhoea are associated with poor nutrient absorption and considerable nutrient losses in the faeces. Both lead to a reduced weight gain or even weight loss, which in some children may cause malnutrition. After diarrhoea most children quickly regain weight and 'catch-up' their previous losses.

Effect of growth status on measles and diarrhoea
The most important mechanisms that bring about increased infection among the severely malnourished are decreased host resistance as a result of selective immunological changes, and changes to intestinal function.

Severe PEM is associated with a high prevalence of measles, presumably as a result of severely decreased host resistance. In moderate or mild PEM, however, there is little evidence of an important role for nutrition in the first stage of the illness; environmental, climatic and behavioural factors seem more important. As complications of measles develop, the role of nutrition becomes more important, especially affecting recovery and duration of disease.

Malnutrition predisposes a child to diarrhoea although different studies have shown contradictory results.

Severely malnourished children are likely to suffer higher measles mortality, although no relation has been found between mild and moderate nutritional status and risk of severe or fatal measles. Environmental factors are probably more important determinants of measles mortality.

(Tomkins, 1986; Tomkins and Watson, 1989; Waterlow and Tomkins, 1992; Briend, 1990; Dugdale *et al.*, 1991; Koster *et al.*, 1981)

To ensure good nutrition, each of the three groups of underlying causes must be adequate and a failure in any aspect will contribute to malnutrition.

Anthropometric status and health risks

Malnutrition and infection
There is a cyclical relationship between malnutrition and infection; infections precipitate malnutrition and malnutrition aggravates the outcome of many infections.

Severe malnutrition increases the incidence, duration and severity of infection. The relationship between moderate malnutrition and infection is less clear, although it has been shown to have a definite effect on the duration of disease (Tomkins and Watson, 1989). Different diseases interact with malnutrition in particular ways. Box 1.6 describes the effect of growth status on measles and diarrhoea, and vice versa.

Not all diseases are precipitated or aggravated by malnutrition. Evidence from field studies during periods of hardship and food insecurity (famine, floods, flight of refugees) shows that malnutrition gives some protection against malaria and that improvements to a previously inadequate diet may precipitate attacks of malaria in those with an existing inactive infection (Murray *et al.*, 1975; Murray *et al.*, 1976; de Waal, 1989c). The growth and multiplication of the malarial parasite is suppressed by certain forms of malnutrition, particularly iron-deficiency anaemia (Murray and Murray, 1977). However, once malaria is able to develop in an undernourished individual, he or she is more likely to die than someone who is well nourished (Tomkins, 1986).

Because of the varying interactions between different diseases and malnutrition, they do not all carry the same mortality risks among malnourished children. In a study in Bangladesh, the relative risk of dying from diarrhoea among severely malnourished as opposed to other children was 17, and was 4.2 for measles and 2.1 for other infectious diseases (Fauveau *et al.*, 1990).

Malnutrition and risk of death
Many field studies suggest there is a range of growth status over which the risk of dying changes only slightly, with a lower threshold below which mortality rises steeply. In most cases severe malnutrition appears to indicate life-threatening risk, whereas risk in moderate malnutrition is less clear. This seems to be true for all indices of malnutrition: weight-for-age, weight-for-height, height-for-age and arm circumference (Gomez *et al.* 1956; Chen *et al.*, 1980; Kielmann and McCord, 1978; Heywood, 1982). Most studies confirm that the relationship between nutritional status and mortality is non-linear and there is a distinct threshold effect.[4] The relationship between malnutrition and mortality in relation

16

to famine and food security is discussed in more depth by Young and Jaspars (in preparation).

The accuracy of different nutritional indices to identify correctly children at risk varies: several studies have shown the sensitivity of weight-for-height to be lower than weight-for-age or height-for-age.[5, 6] Studies in Bangladesh and one in Senegal show that mid-upper arm circumference is the most effective discriminator of mortality risk (Alam *et al.*, 1989; Briend and Zimicki, 1986; Briend *et al.*, 1987; Briend *et al.*, 1989b).

The strength of the association between growth status and mortality risk differs between studies. In Bangladesh, children who were severely malnourished using the weight-for-age index (<60 per cent WFA), experienced a two-fold higher mortality risk over a 12-month follow-up period compared with their well-nourished counterparts (>75 per cent WFA) (Chen *et al.*, 1980). In contrast, a study in Tanzania which used the same cut-off points for the same follow-up period, found severely malnourished children were eight times more likely to die than those categorized as normal (Yambi *et al.*, 1991).

These differences in the strength of association and the discriminating power of nutritional indices are partly caused by differences in the study design, in particular the age groups included in each study and length of follow up after the initial measurements. The size of the mortality risk associated with stunting and wasting partly depends on the age groups selected for study. Infants and younger children experience higher mortality rates which decline as they get older.[7]

---

[4] Not all prospective studies have found a significant association between malnutrition and mortality or a threshold effect. Two studies report an overall linear relationship where the risk of death decreased constantly with improvement in nutritional status (Yambi *et al.*; 1991, Briend and Zimicki, 1986). Two other studies: one in a rural town in East Zaire (Kasongo Project Team, 1983), and the other in urban and rural areas of Guinea Bissau (Smedman *et al.*, 1987), both failed to find an association between nutritional status and mortality, possibly because measles epidemics during the field studies masked the association.

[5] *Sensitivity* is the proportion of those who actually die who are classified by the given nutritional index as malnourished.

[6] One study during a period of drought in rural Malawi found a strong relationship between weight-for-height and mortality; even modestly decreased weight-for-height (between 0 and -1 Z scores) almost doubled the risk of dying, and for children less than -2 the risk was increased fivefold (Lindskog *et al.*, 1988).

[7] For given values of nutritional status measured by weight-for-age, the mortality risk significantly decreased with the child's age (Kielmann and McCord, 1978; Katz *et al.*, 1989; Alam *et al.*, 1989). In contrast, the relative risk associated with moderate to severe wasting (<80 per cent weight-for-height) progressively increased after the second year of life (Katz *et al.*, 1989). Sommer and Loewenstein (1975), found little or no effect of age on mortality in the case of moderate wasting (76 per cent to 83 per cent arm circumference-for-height), but the possibility of greater mortality rates for severe wasting (less than 75 per cent arm circumference-for-height) at older ages.

The pattern of growth failure is also age specific: wasting is more common between the ages of approximately six months and two years, while stunting is rare before two years of age. Most prospective studies of malnutrition and mortality in individuals were undertaken in situations of chronic nutritional problems, where stunting was more common than wasting. In times of acute food insecurity when rates of malnutrition rise, the proportional increases of wasting are greater among older children than among younger children (Kloth *et al.*, 1976; Seaman *et al.*, 1978).

Anthropometry is most effective at identifying shorter-term mortality that occurs within three months of the anthropometric measurements (Sommer and Loewenstein, 1975; Kielmann and McCord, 1978; Bairagi, 1987; Briend *et al.*, 1987).

The more important reason for differences between studies, apart from methodological differences, are the varying patterns of morbidity and growth failure in the different locations. These are determined by a wide range of environmental and social influences, which are specific to a particular location and often fluctuate according to seasonal events or activities.

The results of these studies suggest that where measles was responsible for a high proportion of deaths, the relationship between malnutrition and mortality was weakened. In two studies where measles was responsible for more than 45 per cent of deaths, no association was found between initial nutritional status and risk of death (Kasongo Project Team, 1983; Smedman *et al.*, 1987). In contrast, a small proportion of deaths were attributable to measles in those studies reporting a strong association between malnutrition and mortality.[8]

In conclusion, the risk of death associated with poor nutritional status is determined largely by the prevailing patterns of morbidity. So, although malnutrition may make children more vulnerable to death, it is social and environmental factors that govern exposure to infectious disease and so influence the risk of mortality associated with a given level of malnutrition.[9]

---

[8] Measles accounted for 3.4 per cent of all deaths in the Iringa study, Tanzania (Yambi *et al.* 1991) and 16.9 per cent of deaths in a study in Bangladesh (Chen *et al.*, 1980). Both found a significant strong association between initial nutritional status and mortality although the strength of the association varied.

[9] Two other important factors which appear to affect mortality risk without necessarily affecting nutritional status, are vitamin A status and breast-feeding. A recent review of 10 vitamin-A supplementation trials concluded that improving the vitamin-A status of young children reduced mortality rates by about 23 per cent (Beaton *et al.*, 1993). Severely malnourished breast-fed children have a lower mortality than similarly malnourished non-breast-fed children (Briend and Bari, 1989), despite no apparent differences in morbidity (Briend, 1992).

Famine, malnutrition and death

Is starvation the main cause of famine deaths?

Starvation, or undernutrition, is rarely one of the reported causes of death in famines, although it is widely assumed to contribute to famine deaths. It is disease that finally kills, and the reported cause of death is attributed to a particular disease identified by its obvious symptoms. Amartya Sen, who developed the entitlement theory of famine, believed that

> many of the deaths reported under dysentery, diarrhoea, and enteric groups of fevers, were in fact starvation deaths. The same holds for several other categories, including the general category of death owing to fever. (Sen, 1981)

This view that starvation is a major underlying cause of death in famines, suggests that as people's entitlements fall, they starve, become malnourished and increasingly susceptible to disease and death. This fits in with the evidence discussed earlier about the rising risk of death associated with severe malnutrition. It is also supported by the evidence collected from refugee and famine-affected populations living in camps, where the prevalence of malnutrition is strongly associated with crude mortality rates. In refugee and famine camps the mortality rates are generally highest during the first months of a camp's existence, when refugees or displaced people have recently arrived (Toole and Waldman, 1990). As conditions improve, falling mortality rates are accompanied by improvements in the nutritional status of the population.

But starvation and malnutrition alone do not fully explain the cause of famine deaths as it is not just the severely malnourished children who die; the vast majority of famine deaths occur among children who are not severely malnourished.

Health crisis—the final stage of famine

Famine mortality is the result of a greater incidence of the (endemic) diseases of normal times, including malaria, diarrhoeal diseases, measles, and acute respiratory tract infections (Dyson, 1991a and 1991b; Sen, 1981; Shears, 1991; de Waal, 1989b and 1989c; Toole and Waldman, 1990). The patterns of morbidity during famine or among refugee-affected populations are often a huge exaggeration of normal seasonal patterns (Dyson, 1991).

So what causes this escalation in morbidity and mortality, apart from an increased prevalence of severe malnutrition? In simple terms, the underlying cause of famine deaths is a deterioration in the local health environment which intensifies exposure to disease and raises disease incidence. This 'health crisis' is precipitated by social disruption and distress migration which often produces spontaneous settlements by the roadside or on the edge of towns. These soon become famine camps, where the weak and vulnerable are concentrated.

Spontaneous settlements are usually crowded, as limited space or shortages of building materials mean that people are crammed into makeshift shelters. Sanitation is usually non-existent and the available water supply is often inadequate. Water quickly becomes contaminated, if it is not already. Many of the locations for such camps are inhospitable: sites which are either ferociously hot and dusty, or liable to flooding during the rainy season. There is probably a complete lack of health facilities as local health centres are already overstretched. The presence of a camp places a growing strain on local resources, and not surprisingly, resentment builds up among the local population.

Survival in a famine camp is very different from survival at home, largely because the health risks are so much greater. Transmission of disease is heightened because of the poor health environment: overcrowding, inadequate water supply, poor sanitation and lack of health facilities. People lack the resources to look after themselves; adequate shelter, water carriers, cooking equipment, blankets, suitable clothes, are all probably in short supply. This increases their chances of getting ill and makes it more difficult to care for the sick.

In many famines, mortality continues to be higher than normal long after the food situation has improved. This is because the impact of social disruption and distress migration on the health environment continues long after the drought and associated food shortages. In past famines, raised mortality in the recovery phase of famine is often due to unusually severe outbreaks of malaria (Dyson, 1991a, 1991b; Whitcombe, in preparation). This occurs when a long period of drought ends with abnormally heavy rains. During the drought, transmission of malaria falls and with it the levels of people's acquired immunity, thereby making people more vulnerable. The heavy rainfall creates conditions ideal for mosquitoes to breed. As the food situation improves, the malnourished gain weight and become more susceptible to malaria. This pattern of famine deaths continuing after

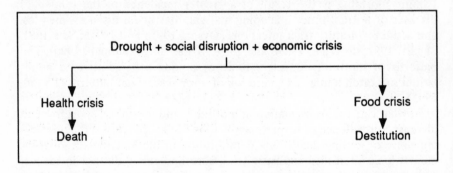

Figure 1.3   Health crisis model of famine (de Waal, 1989a)

20

the worst of the starvation is over has been widely reported in both African and Asian famines.

Alex de Waal (1989a) developed the 'health crisis model' of famine mortality, explaining that people die of disease during famine, without starvation contributing to any deaths.

This extreme view that nutrition or lack of food plays no role in famine mortality ignores the large body of evidence that links severe malnutrition with raised mortality. Waal argues that the prevalence of severe malnutrition may be abnormally high during famine, but it still only includes a small proportion of the total population, and deaths among this group do not usually account for the greater proportion of excess deaths.

It is the combined action of morbidity and malnutrition that leads to famine deaths. In the later stages of famine, a poor health environment intensifies exposure to infection, while malnutrition increases the incidence, duration and severity of infection. A detailed review of the relationship between malnutrition, morbidity and mortality in situations of food insecurity and famine is found in Young and Jaspars (1995).

So who is at greater risk of dying during famine? In normal times infants, very young children and the elderly suffer the highest mortality rates, and in famine they also die in the largest numbers. But researchers have shown that it is older children and adults who suffer the largest proportional increase in mortality (Dyson, 1991). The reason for this is not entirely clear but it could be something to do with the possibility that wasting is associated with greater mortality risks among older children (during famine older children suffer a larger proportional increase in wasting than younger children), or that older children no longer have the added protection of breastfeeding, or that older children in relief camps do not benefit from the fortified supplementary foods given to younger children (Young and Jaspars, 1995).

Starvation and death—the changing relationship

Earlier in this chapter, it was explained that there is a threshold of nutritional status below which mortality risk rises steeply. Above this threshold the risk is less. This threshold has often been found to correspond to the cut-off point for severe malnutrition, but varies according to the social and environmental conditions that determine patterns of morbidity.

Most studies investigating the relationship between malnutrition and risk of death have been done in settled populations under normal conditions, when rates of wasting are relatively low. Little is known about the relative role of moderate malnutrition to morbidity and mortality in famine, when rates of wasting are raised. A poor health environment which causes greater exposure to infection is likely to raise the threshold of nutritional status associated with an increased risk of dying. In a famine camp, moderately malnourished as well as severely malnourished children may be at risk of dying because of the greater exposure to disease. Conversely,

21

among people living at home in a healthy environment an increase in wasting may not be associated with excess mortality.

The interaction between malnutrition and morbidity means the relationship between starvation and death is likely to change in different contexts and with the development of different stages of famine. Box 1.7 gives examples of this changing relationship in relation to food security and famine.

Box 1.7   Examples of the changing relationship between malnutrition and mortality

In southern Ethiopia the mortality rate for a given rate of malnutrition was proportionately higher among children living in relief shelters than in the traditional pastoralist and agro-pastoralist communities (Lindtjorn, 1990).

In a three-year study of more than 5 000 children in southern Ethiopia, there was a rapid decline in nutritional status in the first half of 1989 and 1991, but not in 1990, which was closely linked to the harvest and food security. The mortality risk associated with any given weight-for-length was in 1989 and 1991 very roughly twice that observed in 1990 (Lawrence *et al.*, 1994).

In Bangladesh in August 1975, the prevalence of malnutrition was still raised following the famine, and at 85 per cent weight-for-height mortality was four times that at 95 per cent weight-for-height. At 75 per cent weight-for-height mortality was around 10 times as high. In October, levels of nutritional status had improved and the effects of low weight-for-height on mortality were much less dramatic than for the same levels of nutritional status during the famine (Bairagi *et al.*, 1985).

Could starvation be a means of survival?

High rates of wasting may occur at the very early stages of famine as well as during the late stages, as a reduction in food intake is an early coping strategy. An increase in wasting early on in the development of famine may not necessarily be associated with excess deaths.

There are many so-called famines where rates of wasting are raised and people do not die as a result. In rural Mali during and after the 1973–4 drought there were no signs of any effect on child mortality (Hill, 1987). In some famines the overall level of mortality actually improved as a result of the hot, dry conditions that brought famine causing a reduction in disease (Dyson, 1993).

But once public health deteriorates, exposure to infectious disease is intensified, and the higher incidence of disease contributes to both excess mortality and also to rising rates of malnutrition.

Model of famine process

These ideas about the relationship between nutrition and famine can be illustrated in a diagram. The framework in Figure 1.4 outlines the early and

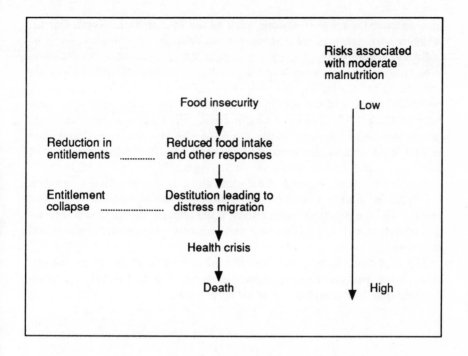

Figure 1.4 Nutritional status, malnutrition and death in famine:
a conceptual framework

late stages of famine. During the early stages of famine, worsening food security (which is equivalent to a reduction in entitlements), prompts people to adopt coping strategies. Eating less or switching to inferior foods is likely to lead to a fall in nutritional status and rising rates of acute malnutrition.

If food insecurity is prolonged and increases in severity, people will be forced to employ strategies that are increasingly threatening to their livelihoods and some may eventually become destitute. This would correspond to a collapse in their entitlements, when they have *no choice* other than to starve. Destitution may prompt distress migration and lead to developing health crises wherever displaced people congregate.

High rates of wasting may occur in both the early and late stages of famine, but the associated risk of dying depends on the prevailing diseases and the intensity of exposure. If public health deteriorates with the advanced stages of famine this probably raises the threshold of anthropometric status associated with increased risk of death.

This means that settled communities suffering high rates of wasting in a healthy environment may not experience death rates raised above normal. In fact, mortality rates may even be lower than normal if drought conditions have reduced transmission of malaria and water-borne diseases. This may account for those situations, such as the case-study in North Darfur, which report high rates of malnutrition without any apparent excess morbidity or mortality.

Nutritional status responds quickly to dietary changes,[10] and so if people voluntarily eat less during the early stages of famine, nutritional status is a sensitive indicator of worsening food security. This issue is explored more fully in Chapter 2. During a health crisis, when exposure to disease is heightened and treatment harder to obtain, the moderately malnourished as well as the severely malnourished are likely to suffer an increased risk of death.

Part 3 of this book expands these ideas and explores how this framework is helpful in gaining a better understanding of the nutritional aspects of famine, and the practical implications of the framework for the interpretation of nutritional data, assessment methods and types of interventions and targeting.

The next two chapters describe the current applications of nutritional surveillance, particularly in relation to early warning, and also the quantitative and qualitative methods that have been used.

---

[10] During the rapid growth phase of recovery from malnutrition, rates of weight gain of 30g/kg/day are frequently seen, which is approximately 10 to 20 times the normal rate of weight gain for a child of the same height (Spady *et al.*, 1976).

CHAPTER 2

Nutritional surveillance for famine early warning

Introduction

Since the African famines of the seventies many countries have developed systems to warn of impending famine and so invoke a response to prevent the worst effects. Nutritional surveillance has been used as a component of early warning systems, which frequently report any available anthropometric data.

Despite problems with its collection and interpretation, anthropometric data are in demand because they provide evidence about the damaging effects of famine on health and the possibility of excess mortality. But it is usually forgotten that the evidence provided by anthropometric data is indirect, and for this reason interpretation is over-simplified: growth failure is assumed to equal starvation and risk of death, while the impact of disease on nutritional status is often ignored.

Unlike most socio-economic variables, nutritional status is relatively easy to measure and considered to be both objective and reliable, partly because it is based on internationally accepted reference standards. But as we shall see in Chapter 3, methods of nutritional surveillance are by no means as foolproof as would first appear.

As part of an early warning system, anthropometric data are usually seen as a safety net, to sound the alarm when other indicators either fail to predict famine or, more likely, fail to get the desired response. In Chad and Mali, nutrition surveys were only undertaken once other agronomic and economic indicators showed a deterioration. The results of the nutrition surveys were used to eliminate 'false positives' from the early warning system (Autier *et al.*, 1989). Anthropometric data are often used first to justify the need for food aid (advocacy), and later to help target this food aid at those most in need.

Anthropometric data have also been used in retrospect to assess the effectiveness of predictive indicators, such as agricultural, climatic or market indicators, at predicting a change in nutritional status. An expert group meeting to discuss 'Uses of Anthropometry' recommended that anthropometric data be used for the 'identification, characterization, and validation of other predictive indicators for future use' (Beaton *et al.*, 1990). This assumes that high rates of malnutrition are what the early warning system is trying to predict and prevent.

Little or no mention is ever made of the use of anthropometric data as a predictive indicator of famine. This is because there is a widely held expert view that anthropometric data are late indicators of famine; in other words, a serious deterioration in nutritional status accompanies, rather than precedes the final phase of famine. This view is summed up by Mason *et al.*, (1984)

> by the time nutritional status is affected, a life-threatening food shortage has progressed dangerously far.

One of the aims of this chapter is to refute the limited view of anthropometry as a late indicator of famine and show why nutritional data can in fact be used as early warning indicators of food insecurity and famine.

The first part of the chapter reviews the practical application of nutritional surveillance, followed by an overview of information systems for monitoring famine and early warning indicators. In the last part of the chapter, we use the knowledge and insights gained about nutrition and famine from Chapter 1 to address the question: can nutritional data be used as an early warning indicator of food security and famine?

Nutritional surveillance

What is nutritional surveillance?

Nutritional surveillance systems gather information about nutrition on a regular basis for a range of purposes, one of which is famine early warning. The World Food Conference in Rome in 1974 marked the beginning of world-wide interest in monitoring nutrition. At the conference, a specific recommendation was made for the co-ordination of surveillance activities of international agencies, and the need for a common approach to planning. The intended aims were international comparisons and global forecasts. Two years later a joint FAO/UNICEF/WHO Expert Committee produced guide-lines on methods and principles of nutritional surveillance (WHO, 1976).

From its first conception, nutritional surveillance raised issues of social and economic access to food. The solution to the problem of malnutrition was thought to lie in 'multi-sectoral' planning, which meant tackling nutritional problems from all perspectives. For many policy makers, fighting nutritional risk was an indirect means of fighting extreme poverty.

Despite these wider considerations of the underlying causes of malnutrition, in practice, the focus of nutritional surveillance has been monitoring anthropometric status of children under five years of age and reporting levels of growth failure.

Nutritional surveillance revolves around a cycle of activities, including assessment and data collection, analysis and interpretation, and most important, appropriate action based on the analysis. UNICEF describes this surveillance cycle as the 'Triple-A' approach, which centres around assessing the problem, analysing its causes and taking action (Figure 2.1).

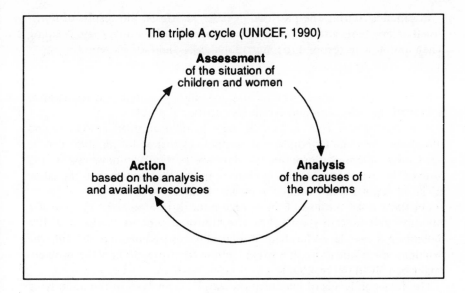

Figure 2.1   The Triple-A cycle (UNICEF, 1990)

The scale of nutritional surveillance is indeterminate, ranging from national surveillance systems to small community surveillance systems which cover a handful of villages.

Previously, the tendency was large-scale country-wide programmes directed by a central unit, but more recently these have declined and there has been a move by UNICEF at least towards decentralized systems which are potentially more cost-effective and better able to identify locally appropriate solutions. The case-study in Part 2 describes the development of a localized system in North Darfur, Sudan.

What practical use is nutritional surveillance?

The methods and results of nutritional assessments usually get much more attention than the actual use of the information, which is really the key to the success of surveillance activities. Collection of data is a meaningless waste of time and money unless the information is put to good effect. In other words, information is for action.

Three broad applications of nutritional surveillance as described by Mason *et al.* (1984) include: policy and planning in the medium to long term; programme management and evaluation; timely[1] warning and intervention for famine prevention (Mason *et al.*, 1984).

---

[1] According to the authors, 'timely' implies that the decision to intervene with a predetermined response is triggered early and in time to prevent deterioration in nutritional status (Mason *et al.*, 1984).

In practice, during the past two decades in Africa, the results of nutritional assessments and surveillance have been used for advocacy, deciding when and how to respond to a nutritional crisis, and for targeting.

Advocacy and political sensitization
Nutrition information is often needed for effective campaigns to sensitize politicians and decision makers about nutritional problems.

The aim of advocacy is to influence the allocation of resources and subsequent actions. Donors are more likely to respond if numbers can be put to a problem. Anthropometric data are particularly newsworthy and forever being quoted on the TV and in the papers in relation to the latest crisis, whether it is in Bosnia, Somalia or Iraq.

On the whole, the use of nutritional data to reinforce the gravity of a situation and so gain the world's attention and support works well. But nutritional surveillance has been criticized for examining and restating the problem of malnutrition rather than getting to grips with how the problem might be solved (Berg, 1991).

The focus on levels of malnutrition with little analysis of the underlying causes of a decline in nutritional status has frequently confused the situation, as food scarcity and famine do not always coincide with a high prevalence of malnutrition. For non-nutritionists, it might be hard to believe that anthropometric data in isolation do not necessarily tell you very much about the nutrition of children, or the community in which they live. Unfortunately it has been given a meaning and importance that is based more on conjecture and speculation than objective fact.

Where there is more than one organization undertaking nutrition surveys there are often long and protracted debates about the reliability and validity of the different results. This technical nit-picking can serve to weaken the role of nutritional data as a tool for advocacy. Methodological problems are explored in Chapter 3 and improving interpretation is addressed in Chapter 6.

Identifying appropriate response strategies
In practice, the typical intervention in response to a high rate of malnutrition in a potential famine situation is the emergency distribution of international food aid. Nutritional surveys are often carried out with the predetermined aim of getting food aid.

The operational approach to emergency food aid is usually mechanistic and 'top-down', as there is often little consultation with local authorities, let alone the local people who are affected. This is illustrated in the Darfur case-study in Part 2.

In recent years there have been many pleas for a wider range of combined strategies and alternative approaches to strengthening food security, which are more in keeping with people's efforts and perceptions of their own needs. But unlike the direct and short-term distribution of food, the strategies needed to sustain and strengthen livelihoods or permanently improve health and nutrition require longer-term commitments to community development, and the agencies involved in emergencies often only have short-term commitments and funding arrangements. Thus the mechanics of large-scale relief programmes discriminate against non-food relief interventions (Duffield, 1994).

More innovative approaches are often beyond the scope of nutritional surveillance as results are often limited to anthropometric data and directed at a single sector, usually the Ministry of Health. Alternatively, the surveillance system may only exist to predict the need for food aid, for example, the nutritional surveillance system in Ethiopia operated by Save the Children Fund (Kelly, 1992).

The varied causes that underlie food shortages and malnutrition are rarely assessed in a systematic way. Yet it is more specific information and a more participatory approach to assessment that are needed to identify the more appropriate response.

Triggering a response
In the past, nutritionists have advised a mechanistic approach to interpreting anthropometric data; a specific action or response is triggered if the prevalence of malnutrition reaches a particular level. In several African countries during the mid-eighties, rates of malnutrition were used to trigger declarations of drought, and specific interventions such as supplementary feeding. In Botswana, for example, the relief strategy was a four-stage system for mobilizing resources which employed trigger levels of prevalence of undernutrition to justify an expansion of drought relief to Stage 2 and Stage 3. (Stage 2 was declared in the event of a prevalence of 40 per cent underweight, Stage 3 was 60 per cent underweight.) The system was confusing and the system of stages beyond Stage 1 was subsequently abandoned (Cogill, 1990).

Some aid agencies have defined famine as a particular level of malnutrition (MSF, 1991). Ethiopian government guide-lines on nutritional survey data and relief provision call for intervention once mean weight-for-length in an area falls below 90 per cent of the reference median (RRC, 1989).

This mechanistic approach makes life easier for technicians and decision makers as it allows them to avoid hard questions about nutritional problems and so evade their responsibility for searching for realistic solutions. Not all nutritionists take this limited view of nutritional data. A group of expert nutritionists have emphasized that changes in prevalence are more important than absolute levels of prevalence, and moreover,

no universal criteria for judging the rate and scale of prevalence change can be offered (Beaton *et al.*, 1990).

In some enlightened circles, the emphasis has shifted from focusing on the actual rates of malnutrition to studying the underlying causes and how they

29

are interlinked. See, for example the UNICEF framework described in Chapter 1, page 13.

Targeting
Targeting focuses the coverage of an intervention on those who are perceived as particularly at risk. This requires a system that will accurately identify who or where they are and provide a simple and fair means of selecting them in preference to others.

Box 2.1 Examples of targeting food assistance using anthropometry

Ghana, 1982
Food assistance was targeted in two stages: first geographically, on the basis of rates of malnutrition among children attending mother and child health centres, and second, according to the nutritional status of individual children. Centres with more than 45 per cent of attending children below 80 per cent of the reference median weight-for-age received double the normal supplementary rations and were the first centres to receive new food shipments. Within these centres food rations were then more precisely targeted at those families whose children were attending the mother and child health programme and found to be malnourished (below 80 per cent weight-for-age) (Shoham, 1987b).

Botswana, pre-1986
Nutritional surveillance data for drought early warning was used for establishing beneficiary groups and target areas for supplementary and special direct feeding programmes. It was also used in some instances for screening individuals for intervention, planning and targeting of other types of relief programme, for example, cash-for-work programmes. Those villages recording higher rates of malnutrition among their children were allocated proportionately more of the funds available (Morgan, 1985).

Ethiopia, 1989 to date
Guide-lines produced by the government's Relief and Rehabilitation Commissions (RRC) recommend immediate emergency intervention (whether food aid, health or other relevant intervention) in any area where the mean weight-for-length falls below 90 per cent of the median weight-for-height, or the percentage less than 80 per cent weight-for-height is more than 10 per cent (RRC, 1989). The RRC also refers to 'temporal' targeting, which relates to the timing of interventions which are intended to occur in advance of an expected decline in nutritional status. A network of nutritional monitoring has been set up in the most vulnerable parts of the country. Save the Children Fund covers the regions of Wollo, Harerghe, parts of northern Shewa and all districts of southern Shewa, having been involved in nutritional surveillance since 1978.

Eastern Sudan, refugee reception centres, 1985–6
Agencies used the weight-for-height nutritional index as the admission and discharge criteria to supplementary and therapeutic 'on-the-spot' feeding programmes. Some used less than 80 per cent weight-for-length (some less than 85 per cent weight-for-length) for admission to supplementary feeding programmes, and less than 70 per cent or 75 per cent weight-for-length for therapeutic programmes (Gibb, 1986).

Geographic targeting identifies entire communities or regions to be covered by an intervention, and selective targeting identifies individuals or households within a community or area according to predetermined criteria, such as socio-economic criteria or anthropometric criteria (see also the section on targeting strategies in Chapter 6, page 120).

Universal support requires a large commitment of resources, and equal distribution of limited resources may mean that only a small proportion reaches the most vulnerable.

Anthropometric data have been used for geographic targeting by selecting those communities or regions suffering higher rates of malnutrition, and therefore considered at greatest 'risk'. They have also been widely used for screening individuals using a nutritional status 'cut-off point' as the criterion. Examples of criteria for targeting food assistance are shown in Box 2.1.

Targeting individual children

In famine and refugee relief operations, supplementary and therapeutic feeding programmes are often targeted at malnourished children using a nutritional index, such as weight-for-height, to screen all children.[2] Those whose nutritional status falls below the agreed cut-off point are admitted to the programme. The objective of these programmes is to target those children at greater physiological risk.

An efficient index for screening individuals should correctly identify a high proportion of those who actually are at risk of dying (high sensitivity), while at the same time it should exclude those children who are not at risk (high specificity) (Habicht, 1982). Sensitivity and specificity are inversely related, as sensitivity increases, specificity decreases.

Levels of sensitivity and specificity have been calculated in several prospective studies of malnutrition and mortality. Even where a relatively high level of sensitivity has been achieved, there are many misclassifications. For example, in rural Bangladesh, an arm circumference cut-off point of fewer than 100mm could identify children who would die within one month with 94 per cent specificity and 56 per cent sensitivity (Briend *et al.*, 1987). In other words, 56 per cent of those children who actually died had a MUAC measurement below 110mm, while 94 per cent of those who survived had a MUAC measurement above 110mm.

Levels of sensitivity and specificity are location specific. Other studies have shown far lower levels of sensitivity than quoted above, particularly for the weight-for-height index. Among children admitted to a hospital in Dhaka, Bangladesh, a weight-for-height cut-off of less than 70 per cent gave a sensitivity of 40 per cent at a level of specificity of 66 per cent (Briend *et al.*, 1986).

---

[2] There have been occasions, such as the 1984–5 famine in Wollo, Ethiopia, when general rations were targeted at those families with malnourished children, as the available food was much less than the estimated need.

Better screening efficiency can be achieved by raising the cut-off and targeting more children, but this reduces the level of specificity (more children are included who are not at risk) and the higher costs incurred by including more children may be prohibitive. Table 2.1 uses the data from Chen *et al.* (1980), to show how raising the weight-for-height cut-off point from less than 70 per cent weight-for-height to less than 80 per cent weight-for-height increases the level of sensitivity from 14.7 per cent to 34.8 per cent, but means targeting nearly nine times as many children.

Table 2.1   Example of the sensitivity and specificity of two cut-off levels of weight-for-height to identify correctly children who die (example adapted from data presented by Chen *et al.*, 1980)

Weight-for-height	Number of children below cut-off	Died Yes	Died No	Sensitivity	Specificity	Number of children above cut-off who are at risk
<80%	641	39	602	34.8%	68.4%	73
<70%	75	11	64	14.7%	96.6%	101

(Total number of children in population = 2 019)

The sensitivity of a nutritional index is likely to change with the advance of famine. In the early stages of famine, when health risks are low, the threshold of nutritional status that corresponds to an increased risk of death is likely to be lower that at the later stages of famine, when a poor health environment has brought about an increased incidence of disease. In other words, in the later stages of famine, moderate malnutrition as well as severe malnutrition may incur a high risk.

Information systems for monitoring famine

What are early warning systems?

Since the African famines of the seventies most but not all countries in the Horn of Africa and the Sahel have national-level early warning systems to predict impending famine and so evoke a response that will prevent it occurring. The idea of an institutional system to warn of impending food crisis is not new; it was implicit in the Famine Codes used by the British in nineteenth-century India and was adopted in the 1920s in Sudan.

The events that early warning systems are trying to predict and the indicators they monitor depend on their view of famine. Chapter 1 described how assumptions about the causes of famine have changed from the belief that famines were caused by food shortages, to the now-accepted view that a failure in people's exchange entitlements is the key issue. In keeping with changing views, early warning systems have shifted their emphasis from monitoring food availability to monitoring people's access to food.

The outcome of famine was previously thought of as acute starvation coupled with excess mortality. The more current views recognize that famine is a long process, the outcome of which includes the erosion of people's livelihoods, destitution and social disruption, but does not necessarily include excess deaths.

Despite these developments, most early warning systems are geared towards preventing mass starvation and death, rather than reducing the economic risks to livelihoods associated with the earlier stages of famine.

In practice, the approach taken by an early warning system is partly influenced by the level of administration at which it operates. The international and national systems generally focus on estimating food deficits in order to predict acute food shortages, and in the event of mass starvation they react by providing emergency relief, invariably food aid.

For example, the principal aim of the Global Information and Early Warning System (GIEWS) run by the the FAO from Rome, is to warn the international aid community and participating national governments of food shortages for food aid planning. Estimates of food surpluses and deficits are made on the basis of the food balance sheet, a tool developed by the FAO and now widely used by national early warning systems.

The early warning system in Botswana mainly depends on rainfall and agricultural data for monitoring crop production and crop deficits (Davies *et al.*, 1991). It also incorporates nutritional surveillance data as the main 'outcome' indicator (Morgan, 1985).

In contrast, the more localized systems often attempt to monitor increased vulnerabilities and risks to livelihoods, by examining the possible causes of food insecurity, as well as trends in food security indicators. The precise information collected by an early warning system with an emphasis on food security is often specific to each particular location and social group, and the significance of any variable is likely to vary from one community to another.

For example, the *Suivi Alimentaire Delta Seno* (SADS) in Mali, is a local-level, decentralized system covering four districts in Mali. The approach of SADS is to focus on how people feed themselves, rather than on how they fail to do so, using a wide variety of socio-economic indicators and qualitative data (Davies *et al.*, 1991).

If the focus of early warning is on livelihoods, rather than starvation and death, there is a broader range of response options which can be implemented long before the final stages of famine. These are intended to support people's own coping strategies and to minimize the damage such strategies may cause. For example, de-stocking programmes are intended to protect

33

livestock owners from any sudden fall in livestock prices on the open market. Work programmes provide a source of cash income, or payment may be in food. Animal feed programmes support the livelihoods of livestock owners by providing animal fodder when there are shortages of grazing.

In practice, several complementary early warning systems based on different principles often operate within the same country or area, and jointly provide a comprehensive early warning system. For example, in Mali the localized SADS system complements the efforts of the national Systèmes d'Alerte Précoce (SAP) system. SADS is food-security oriented, which complements the efforts of the famine-oriented SAP which recommends food aid distributions (Davies *et al.*, 1991).

Early warning indicators

The growth in famine early warning systems has been accompanied by a search for the best indicators to monitor food security and famine. Rainfall and agricultural data are generally regarded as the only genuine early indicators of approaching famines (Beaton *et al.*, 1990). Market indicators are also usually seen as early indicators, although some view them as concurrent or even late indicators of famine (Mason *et al.*, 1984; de Waal, 1988). Distress migration and malnutrition are generally considered to be late indicators, associated with the final stage of famine. Although, as we are about to explain, we disagree that malnutrition is a late indicator of famine.

Food production data
All early warning systems collect information on food production and availability. The two most common indicators used are rainfall and agricultural production data, which are usually based on crop assessment and pest monitoring.

Food production data are needed for food balance sheets, which aim to calculate the expected food deficit by comparing food supplies (opening stocks, imports, production) with disposals (domestic use, exports, closing stocks). Food balance sheets suffer from several limitations as they do not include all crops, for example, off-season and root crops, and are unable to identify who is affected, how many people, where they are and when they will require relief (Davies *et al.*, 1991).

Socio-economic data
Early warning systems with a food-security orientation monitor socio-economic indicators such as market indicators and coping strategies. Market indicators include staple grain prices and livestock prices. These are often combined in a 'terms of trade' index used as an indicator of people's exchange entitlements. For example, the goat/millet terms of trade shows how much millet may be purchased through the sale of one goat. The relevant terms of trade depend on the local production system.

34

Examples of coping strategies that may be monitored by early warning systems are shown in Table 2.2. In theory, if the types of coping strategies and their sequence of use are known, it should be possible to assess a decline in food security and predict famine in advance (D'Souza, 1989). In practice this is an extremely complex and difficult task.

Table 2.2 Examples of coping strategies that can be monitored for famine early warning

o Sales of livestock or other assets that cause a fall in market prices
o Demand for credit or other loans
o Migration of family members in search of work
o Dietary changes—substitution of a less-preferred but cheaper staple, the collection of wild foods
o Sales of wild foods

Coping strategies must be interpreted with care because they are so specific to a particular time, place and group of people. For example, there are many different reasons for migration; migration of a single household member for work is often a regular occurrence or an early response to food insecurity, whereas distress migration of the whole household is often the final response once the household has become destitute.

Coping strategies are more straightforward to monitor in those communities which make use of certain coping strategies only occasionally, say in periods of drought or food insecurity. Their meaning is less clear among rural communities who face a yearly food gap and have to use coping strategies on a regular basis. As food insecurity worsens the actual strategies they use may stay the same but the reason for using them and the timing of their use may change. The continued use of the same coping strategies may disguise a fundamental change in the local environment, or even mask a collapse of livelihood systems.

Can we predict famines from monitoring nutritional status?

Anthropometric data are not used to predict famine because they are usually perceived as an outcome or late indicator of famine. The main argument for malnutrition being a late indicator of famine is that people do not cut back on food until they are forced to at a late stage of famine. Added delays are caused by the lag period between eating less and weight loss, and also by the time-consuming methods of collecting anthropometric data.

But there is little or no practical evidence to support the idea that people do not reduce their food consumption until they absolutely have to; rather the opposite appears to be true.

Seasonal changes in nutrition

In Africa and Asia, researchers have widely observed that weight-for-height and weight-for-age fluctuate according to the seasons because of seasonal changes in food security, patterns of disease, activity and childcare practices (de Garine and Kappert, 1988; Longhurst and Payne, 1981; Teokul et al., 1986; Loutan and Lamotte, 1984).

In most rural areas in Africa there are periods every year when household food security is under stress. Seasonal food production affects the availability of food, the market price of food and the demand for agricultural labour. Just before the harvest, agricultural work is at its peak, while at the same time stocks from last year's harvest are nearly used up and cash is running out. Shortages of food usually coincide with higher market prices, which fall following the harvest. Women, who are often responsible for much of the agricultural work, have less time available for preparing meals and child care. Anticipating hard work, mothers wean their infants or, if they continue to breast-feed, may only be able to do so less regularly. This lean period before the harvest is known as the hungry season because of nutritional stress.

The hungry season coincides with the rainy season, especially where the rains are concentrated into a single season and people are dependent on a single staple crop with little opportunity for other work. The rainy season may also coincide with an increased incidence of infectious disease, especially diarrhoea, respiratory diseases and malaria.

The harvest replenishes food stores, and cash may be raised through the sale of food crops. Food intake recovers in both quantity and quality, and less illness means lower mortality. Despite a severe lean period and failure to gain weight, or even weight loss, the overall weight gain of children over the year as a whole may be satisfactory (Loutan and Lamotte, 1984).

The pattern of seasonal changes in anthropometric status varies. In general, among agricultural groups there is distinct growth faltering during the rainy season, and weight gain is maximal shortly after the end of the harvest (Teokul et al., 1986). In contrast, among pastoralists the hot dry season is often the time of weight loss and growth faltering. Once the rainy season is under way, there is plenty of water and feed for animals; milk and other products are plentiful and labour needs are low. Later in the hot dry season food and water are less plentiful, and it is hard work to ensure that animals receive enough food and water to survive. The situation is complicated by the farming that some pastoralist groups do during the wet season.

Seasonal shortages of food are usually greatest where most food is from local production and from a single harvest.[3] Perhaps insufficient is

---

[3] Schofield (1974) analysed a number of village studies, and found that villages with a bimodal distribution of rainfall have less seasonal variation in their diet, although seasonal stresses still exist.

produced to last the entire year, or crops do not store well because of high humidity or poorly storing varieties. In semi-arid climates, millets and sorghums are grown, which store well, often for several years. This enables people to cope not only with seasonal variation but also with inter-annual variation, which is common in these areas.

When do people decide to eat less and lose weight?

Drought results in an unusually severe hungry season followed by a harvest which is well below average. Dietary changes are one of the earliest strategies rural people adopt:

> the observation that households reduce their food consumption levels in the early stages of a coping strategy and not just in the later stages suggests that part of the strategy of coping may be to become undernourished (Corbett, 1988).

Box 2.2   Examples of dietary change as an early response to food insecurity

In western Rajasthan, India, people reduced their food intake soon after a drought and associated period of scarcity. This was at the same time as the sale of inventories (home-produced goods and stocks; fuelwood, dung cakes, timber, mats, ghee, pickles, spun wool, clothing, etc), but long before the mortgaging and sales of assets (Jodha, 1975).

In Wollo, Ethiopia, in 1984, reduced consumption and austerity was one of the earliest responses to the food crisis (Rahmato, 1988). Cheaper staple grains, including sorghum, maize and barley were substituted for the preferred cereal 'tef' and also wheat, as an early response to the threat of food shortage. These were prepared without an accompanying sauce or stew, which was cheaper and easier to prepare (Rahmato, 1988; Kelly, 1992).

Amongst agro-pastoralists in Kordofan, Sudan, early in the famine of the 1980s, milk and milk products were no longer available to women and children. Lack of pasture around the village had forced men to extend animal migration routes (Reily, 1991).

In north-east Kenya, among the Turkana, milk contributed 93 per cent of the total diet in the wet season, but only 19 per cent of the diet during the late dry season. In the dry season blood was relied upon as a substitute for milk, and livestock off-take increased. Consumption of cereals and also wild foods became more important (Galvin, 1988).

Among the Boran in Kenya, milk consumption was reduced during drought due to the dispersal of herds and their decreased milk yields, while the consumption of grain products increased (Fleuret, 1986).

Among Taita farmers in marginal areas of south-eastern Kenya, meat consumption increased during drought because of high mortality among livestock. Many households fasted at midday or evening meals preparing no food at all during the drought (Fleuret, 1986).

Not only the amount of food consumed, but also the type of foods eaten and the quality may change early on in the famine process, and could adversely affect nutritional status. Examples of dietary change in response to periods of food insecurity are given in Box 2.2. Coping strategies are discussed in Chapter 1, page 6.

The dietary changes that occur during the hungry season are indicative of the early stages of a long drought. Following a normal harvest, there is a rapid recovery in weight, but if the harvest is poor there is still likely to be some improvement in nutritional status although not a complete recovery. The onset of the following hungry season may be earlier than usual and more severe. After drought the effects of the hungry season become increasingly difficult to reverse.

Two examples of the impact of drought and famine on nutritional status are shown in Figures 2.2 and 2.3. Figure 2.2 shows the nutritional status of 1 178 children under five years from a rural area of Malawi. Food security, based on subsistence farming, was badly affected by the poor rainy season

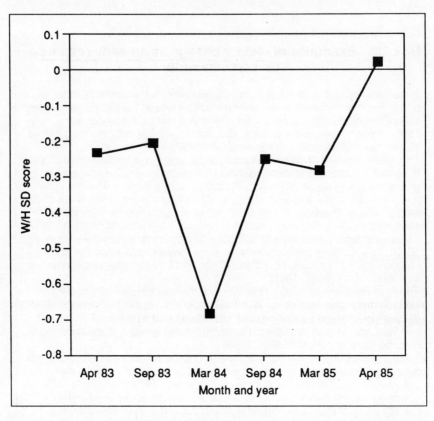

Figure 2.2 Average weight-for-height SD scores of children under five in a rural area of Malawi from 1983 to 1985 (Lindskog *et al.*, 1988)

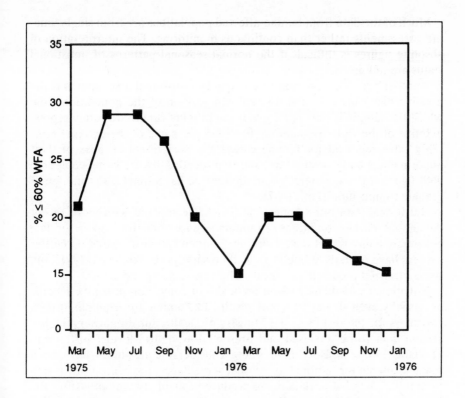

Figure 2.3 Percentage of severely malnourished children from 1975 to 1976 in Matlab, Bangladesh (less than or equal to 60% weight-for-age) (Bairagi *et al.*, 1985)

of 1984. This drought period coincided with a drop in nutritional status (Lindskog *et al.*, 1988).

Figure 2.3 shows the prevalence of severely malnourished children aged one through four years from 12 villages in Matlab, Bangladesh, from April 1975 to December 1976. Usually November through to February is a good season because of the harvest of the main crop (aman paddy), but 1974–5 was a famine period, which is reflected in the higher figures of severely malnourished children in Figure 2.3 (Bairagi *et al.*, 1985).

Can nutritional surveillance methods adequately reflect these changes?

Problems with nutritional surveillance methods often hinder the use of anthropometry as an early warning indicator, in particular the patchiness of data as only a few data points are available, and the delays in data collection and reporting.

Much of the data from famine-affected populations are from single 'one-off' assessments rather than continuous monitoring. The interpretation of absolute figures is difficult if the normal seasonal patterns of nutritional status are unknown.

Another problem common to emergency nutritional assessments is the possible bias caused by the unusual composition of the population from which the sample is drawn. People living in relief camps are rarely representative of the wider population. For example, some of the extreme mortality rates reported for famine camps are exceptional because of their abnormal age and sex structure, and their death rates are being compared with figures for the general population which has a quite different demographic composition (Hill, 1987).

Nutritional data often appear out of date compared with more recent data about market conditions or rainfall because of the time taken for data collection, analysis and report writing. Sampling methods based on cluster surveys have been developed to speed up surveys (Binkin *et al.*, 1991), but the centralized processing of results often slows down the analysis.

Nutritional surveillance based on health or clinic administrative records are usually even slower to report results. In Zambia, for example, it took two years for the results of the Ministry of Health nutritional surveillance system data to be analysed and presented at central level (Borton and Shoham, 1985). In Botswana, where considerable resources have been made available for national nutritional surveillance, the central processing of monthly data led to data being produced roughly two months after the time of weighing (Morgan, 1985). As a result these systems are reporting too late to be of use in predicting changes in food security.

Despite these methodological problems there have been situations in which the results of nutritional surveillance have shown that nutritional status is indeed an early indicator of a decline in food security. In Ghana, for example, the results of growth monitoring indicated a developing crisis 18 months before the government emergency declaration and request for food aid in 1983 (Shoham, 1987b). In Wollo, Ethiopia, following a failure of the 'meher' harvest (the harvest following the second rains) in late 1987, mean weight-for-length of children was on average 1.5 percentage points lower than the previous year. This decrease took place before, or alongside, food price rises and before sale of assets, which indicates that anthropometric status could have been used as an early indicator (Kelly, 1992). Our own case-study of nutritional surveillance in North Darfur also shows that nutritional status is a sensitive indicator of food security (see Part 2).

These examples of unseasonal changes in nutritional status from Ethiopia, Ghana, Malawi, Bangladesh, Ghana and Sudan support our view that eating less is an early response to seasonal and unseasonal food insecurity, and is rapidly reflected in nutritional status. We conclude that a decline in nutritional status can be an early indicator of famine, providing that the seasonal patterns of nutritional status, disease and food security are known and well understood, and that delays in data collection are minimized.

This last proviso about methods of nutritional surveillance is expanded and explored in the next chapter and again in Chapter 6.

CHAPTER 3

Methods of nutritional assessment and surveys

Expensive nutritional status surveys have become so common over the years that people can rightly ask whether we now are getting any kind of return at all on an investment in more surveys, at least as they have traditionally been undertaken—often measuring for the sake of measuring

(Berg, 1991).

Ten years on from the 'great Sahel drought' we should perhaps be looking for methods of data collection, analysis and use, which are practicable within the existing means and structures of the poorest developing countries; not constructing grandiose theoretical frameworks with demands for data far beyond the means of poor countries and which even if collected would not be likely to lead to the best decisions

(Seaman, J., 1984 Book reviews, 'Nutritional Surveillance', Mason *et al.*, *Disasters*, 8/4/84).

Introduction

The main objective of nutritional surveillance methods is to measure the nutritional status of children under five years of age, using nutritional indices, like weight-for-height. Nutritional indices are known as nutritional indicators when they are used to assess the nutritional status of communities or larger populations. Nutritional indicators are used either to provide a direct measure of nutritional status and malnutrition among children, or they are used as indirect indicators or proxies for other factors of interest which are more difficult to measure than nutritional status.

Often the nutritional status of children is taken to reflect the nutritional status of the wider population. In addition, the nutritional status of children serves as a marker for the processes that contributed to malnutrition, such as the changing food security situation or the seasonal patterns of infectious disease. In famine situations, the prevalence rate of malnutrition is understood by many to reflect the changing risks of disease and death in the population; as rates of malnutrition rise so does excess mortality.

Anthropometric data are obtained from formal sample surveys or from existing growth monitoring data collected by mother and child health clinics. Where the MCH system is undeveloped or the local infrastructure is generally weak, surveys form the basis of nutritional surveillance.

Apart from monitoring nutritional status, other objectives may be specified, such as identifying the underlying causes of malnutrition or the most 'at-risk' groups. But the system will be designed primarily around the quantitative assessment of nutritional status, and other data collection has to fit in around this. Additional quantitative information about the child is easily gathered at the same time as the anthropometric assessment. This might include age, sex, symptoms of disease, number of siblings, etc. Household questionnaires are more time-consuming to complete and so unsuited for regular surveillance.

Community-level data, such as market prices, are often routinely monitored by nutritional surveillance systems. Surveillance systems sometimes distinguish between 'outcome' indicators like anthropometric indices, and 'process' or 'risk' indicators which lead to growth failure.

In contrast to formal survey techniques which determine how much or how many, a wide range of qualitative methods have been developed for gathering information relevant to relief and development. These are useful for learning about attitudes and behaviours, causal relationships and the process of change. The several apparently distinct approaches share basic principles and often use similar techniques. Rapid rural appraisal (RRA) is one of the original approaches, although it is no longer always rapid.

Qualitative methods are potentially of great value for nutritional surveillance because of their ability to explore the underlying causes of malnutrition and reveal much that was previously unknown. Moves to adopt these new approaches have been slow, partly because any new methods have to fit in with the collection of anthropometric data.

This chapter reviews the recommended procedures for anthropometric surveys and also the wide array of qualitative approaches to collecting information. The purpose of this review is to outline options for overcoming many of the problems associated with the standard approach to nutritional assessments.

The best solution is usually found in a mix of complementary methods, the choice of which depends on the objectives of surveillance, the available resources, including time and personnel, and the local circumstances.

Anthropometric methods

Anthropometric sample surveys measure the anthropometric status of a selected sample of children. Each child's measurements are transformed into their anthropometric status (SD score or percentage of the reference median). The measurement of growth failure is described in Chapter 1, page 10.

Survey coverage

A sample of children is drawn at random from all children in the population of interest. This might be a single village or camp, several villages, an urban area or a much larger region. Often it is difficult to obtain reliable information to produce a sampling frame, which is an accurate list of every child in the population.[1]

The coverage of the sampling frame depends on the objectives of the surveillance system. World-wide interest in nutritional surveillance in the late seventies generated many national nutrition surveys, which were organized centrally by a small group of technicians. These large-scale surveys were an expensive undertaking and took months if not years to complete. Processing results was often too slow to be of any use other than in long-term planning and policy making. In 1987 WHO compiled data from nearly 50 national surveys completed since 1975 (WHO, 1987).

In more recent years there has been a move away from one-off large-scale surveys towards local-level systems, which continuously monitor

---

Box 3.1   Advantages of sentinel site surveillance

Better understanding of differences	Geographical differences in anthropometric status are readily apparent. National nutrition surveys often produce data that are aggregated over wide areas which masks the nutritional diversity of the population.
More timely data	Sentinel sites reduce the data 'turn-around' time . Results are immediately available at the site itself, and can be more widely distributed shortly afterwards.
Depth rather than breadth of information	Fewer sites are monitored for sentinel site surveillance than for surveys representative of wider areas. This allows more time to be spent in individual sites collecting a wide variety of information about causes of malnutrition.
Minimize costs	Costs of surveillance are kept down by reducing the number of survey sites. Costly mobile survey teams are not required as data are collected by local teams and then sent to a co-ordinating unit at a higher level of administration.
Opportunity for developing a more participatory approach to assessment	Local people assess their own nutritional problems and decide how best they can be solved. A participatory assessment is the starting point for a participatory development programme.

---

[1] Census data are often unreliable or out-of-date, and other sources of population data are often biased, for example, tax records sometimes underestimate the size of the population, while records from food distributions are more likely to overestimate population numbers.

anthropometric status. This is partly because of the huge expense of large-scale surveys, but also because the needs for information at a local level differ from the use of data at national level.

Alongside the move towards more decentralized systems has been increasing interest in monitoring a limited number of sentinel sites as an alternative to selecting a sample that is representative of the entire population. Sentinel site surveillance has been used successfully for health planning in Mexico and Central America (Andersson *et al.*, 1989). The many advantages of sentinel sites over wider coverage are summarized in Box 3.1.

Cross-sectional or longitudinal?
Sample surveys may be cross-sectional, which provide a snapshot in time of the nutritional situation, or longitudinal, which monitor anthropometric status trends among the same sample of children over a period of time. To show seasonal changes, cross-sectional surveys may be repeated at intervals.

Maintaining the representativeness of a longitudinal sample poses particular problems. Over time some children drop out for one reason or another, perhaps their families leave the area, or the children become sick or die or perhaps they find the regular commitment too inconvenient. A problem unique to nutrition surveys is the increasing age of the children in the sample, as children grow older the cumulative effects of stunting become more obvious and they are less likely to be wasted than younger children.

Simple random sampling, systematic sampling and cluster sampling

There are several ways of selecting a sample. Simple random sampling ensures that each child or sampling unit has the same chance (probability) of being selected. Individual children are chosen from the sampling frame by taking random numbers and selecting the child corresponding to that number.

Alternatively, systematic sampling does not require a sampling frame, as children are selected 'systematically' at equal intervals, say every tenth child registered at the health clinic or encountered during a house-to-house survey. The size of the sampling interval is equal to the total population divided by the sample size. A random number between one and the sampling interval is used to select the first child. Say, for example, the interval size was 90, and the first child was number 39, the second child would be number 129 (90+39).

Simple random sampling and systematic sampling are suitable for small surveys, or where households are arranged in organized lines or blocks. For surveys covering a large population, cluster sampling is usually more appropriate. Cluster sampling selects children in groups or 'clusters'. Each cluster usually has the same number of children.

Cluster sample design
Selection of a cluster sample is often done in two stages. In the first stage, all sample sites are listed with their population size and the cumulative

population. The total number of sites is greater than the required number of clusters, and clusters are selected systematically at equal intervals in the cumulative population column. This is known as assigning 'probability proportional to size', which ensures that all children have an equal chance of being selected, irrespective of whether they come from large or small villages.

The second stage of sampling involves selecting the required number of children from each selected site or cluster. The results from the individual clusters are combined to give an estimate for the whole population.[2]

Cluster sampling is more convenient than simple random sampling, because a cluster design reduces the distance travelled by the survey team. The number of sites visited for a cluster survey is equal to the number of clusters, unlike a simple random design where every child could be located in a different place. Another advantage of cluster sampling is that less information is needed to construct the sampling frame; all that is needed is a list of all communities and a rough estimate of their size.

A cluster design often recommended for nutrition assessments is based on a sample size of 30 clusters of 30 children (Binkin *et al.*, 1991). This is a variant of the cluster design traditionally used for the assessment of immunization coverage which is based on 30 clusters of seven children. This standard design is favoured by the WHO and has been adopted for a range of other purposes, including estimates of disease incidence, service coverage and health service needs.

The reason why the number of children per cluster is increased from seven to 30 for a nutrition survey is to ensure that roughly the same number of houses are visited during a nutritional survey as would be visited during an immunization survey[3] (Miller *et al.*, 1977). There are many examples of cluster designs used for nutrition surveys in which more or fewer than 30 clusters have been used.

Sample design and precision of results

The sample design affects the precision of the results, which is the closeness of the sample results to the results had all children in the population been measured. Precision of results is affected by the choice of sample design, sample size and whether the sample is cross-sectional or longitudinal.

The confidence interval is a statistical measure of the precision of the results. It shows with 95 per cent probability the range in which the true

---

[2] Practical guide-lines and examples of cluster sampling for nutrition surveys are described in an Oxfam practical guide: *Food scarcity and Famine, Assessment and Response*, by H.Young, 1992.

[3] Immunization coverage surveys usually include children under one year of age, whereas nutrition surveys usually measure children under five years of age, and so more children must be included in each cluster of the nutrition survey in order that more houses are visited.

population figure is found (the result had all children been measured). It allows you to make statements like 'the prevalence of malnutrition lies between 11.2 per cent and 17.9 per cent (with 95 per cent probability)'.

The sample size influences the size of the confidence interval; the larger the sample size the narrower the confidence interval. With a cluster sample design, the number of clusters, not the number of children, is the main determinant of the size of the confidence interval. Fewer clusters widens the confidence interval.

Cluster sampling is not as statistically reliable as simple random sampling as children within clusters are often more similar in their anthropometric status than children between clusters. This may mean that the results from individual clusters vary considerably. Such differences are often exaggerated in the development of famine, when the prevalence of malnutrition is high and pockets of malnutrition develop where food security is worse or where there is an outbreak of infectious disease.

To compensate for this clustering effect, sample size for a cluster design is increased (usually doubled), and a correction factor is applied when calculating the confidence interval. Traditionally, a correction factor of two is routinely used although an accurate correction factor should be worked out by calculating the 'design effect', based on experience of previous surveys of similar design and subject matter.

The design effect compares the result obtained with a cluster sample with the result obtained by treating the same data as if they were a simple random sample. This shows the performance of the cluster design, or in other words, how suitable the cluster design is in the particular context. A large design effect produces a bigger correction factor and so increases the width of the confidence interval. In practice, few field surveys in situations of food insecurity and famine estimate the design effect.

Longitudinal surveys measure changes with greater precision than a series of independent samples of the same size. Smaller longitudinal samples are therefore adequate for obtaining the same degree of precision as a larger cross-sectional sample.

Abandoning sampling!

Sometimes it is easier to measure all children present rather than select a sample. This has its advantages, as there is no need to calculate the confidence intervals because the result is specific to the population. Because less knowledge of statistics is required, there is a greater role for local field-workers in the analysis. Expert nutritionists or statisticians are not needed for the preliminary analysis of the results. The inclusion of all children in the survey, rather than a selected few, may be easier to understand and therefore more acceptable to the local community.

Great efforts are needed to ensure that all children have in fact been measured, as some are bound to be absent or unable to participate, either because they are unwell or do not want to co-operate in the survey. Missing data may bias the results.

Analysis and presentation of anthropometric data

The anthropometric status of each child is calculated using an appropriate nutritional index. For population assessments of anthropometric status, SD scores should be used rather than percentage of the median, because SD scores succeed in standardizing the measurements for all indices and age groups.[4]

Common statistics for summarizing these results are shown in Box 3.2. The most popular way of expressing anthropometric results is the prevalence rate of malnutrition (growth failure), which is the percentage of children whose nutritional status falls below a standard cut-off point. Increasingly, nutritionists are favouring the use of mean nutritional status over the use of proportions below a cut-off. This is principally because smaller sample sizes are needed to show a significant change in the mean nutritional status, compared with differences in the prevalence (Briend *et al.*, 1989a).

Because the mean anthropometric status is based on all children in the sample, it can be estimated with greater precision than the prevalence rate, which is based on a smaller number of children. This means that larger samples are needed to demonstrate significant differences between the prevalence of different samples than would be required to show a significant difference between means (*ibid.*).

The statistical difference between two means is largely a function of sample size. Changes in the mean may give a good indication of changes in food security, but do not necessarily correspond to important physiological differences, such as risk of disease and death. In practice, a significant difference in the prevalence of malnutrition may be more meaningful than a significant difference in the mean anthropometric status. This is because the relationship between anthropometric status and mortality is *not* linear; there is a threshold of anthropometric status below which the risk of death increases markedly (for more details see Chapter 1).

For details of how to calculate the statistics in Box 3.2 see Young, 1992.

---

[4] Percentage of the median is not standardized for all indices. For example, weight in healthy, well-fed individuals varies more than height; for this reason an SD score of –2 is roughly equivalent to 80 per cent weight-for-height, but to 90 per cent height-for-age.

Percentage of the median is also age dependent as it has different meanings (SD values) at different height values. The 80 per cent curve does not follow the reference curve.

Box 3.2   Useful statistics for summarizing the results of anthropometric surveys

The prevalence of malnutrition: the prevalence rate of children whose anthropometric status falls below the cut-off point (–2 SD scores or 80 per cent of the reference median weight-for-height).

Standard error of the prevalence and confidence interval: a measure of variation in the sample between sampling units or clusters.

The mean: the average anthropometric status of all children measured (the average SD score or average percentage of the median).

Standard error of the mean and confidence interval (cluster survey): a measure of variation in the average anthropometric status of sampling units or between each cluster.

Distribution curves
Distribution curves of Z scores give a complete picture of the nutritional status of the whole population which can be compared with that of the reference population. To calculate a frequency distribution curve, the range of Z scores from –5.49 to +3.5 is broken down into a number of intervals and the proportion of children within each interval is calculated. This data is used to plot the frequency distribution curve (Box 3.3) (Waterlow *et al.*, 1977).

Computer software is available to calculate the Z score and percentage of the median for each child, and also to calculate summary statistics and plot distribution curves.[5]

The frequency distribution curve shows the nutritional status of all the children in the sample, whereas the prevalence of malnutrition focuses on a small proportion of children at the lower end of the distribution curve.

Age groups
Where possible, anthropometric results should be presented separately for age groups under and over 24 months (less than 85cm). At least two to three hundred children are needed for each age group category. The main reason for distinguishing between the nutritional status of different age groups is because the pattern of growth failure varies with age. Wasting is

---

[5] Software in common use:
  ANTHRO, Sullivan, K.M. and Gorstein, J., 1990. ANTHRO Version 1.01: software for calculating pediatric anthropometry. Centers for Disease Control, Atlanta and World Health Organization, Geneva.
  EPI-INFO, Dean, A.G., Dean, J.A., Burton, A.H. and Dicker, R.C., 1990. Epi-info Version 5: a word processor, database, and statistics program for epidemiology on microcomputers. USD, Inc, Stone Mountain, Georgia.
  EPI-NUT, Coulombier, D., Dionisius, J.P. and Desve, G., 1991. Epi-nut Version 1.0: software for analysis of nutrition surveys. Epicentre, 8 rue St. Sabin, 75011 Paris.

Box 3.3 Calculating the frequency distribution and plotting distribution curves

Z-score range	Sample distribution Weight-for-height %	Reference distribution %
–5.49 to –5.0	0.0	0.0
–4.99 to –4.5	0.0	0.0
–4.49 to –4.0	0.0	0.0
–3.99 to –3.5	0.0	0.0
–3.49 to –3.0	1.4	0.1
–2.99 to –2.5	5.5	0.5
–2.49 to –2.0	13.2	1.7
–1.99 to –1.5	18.3	4.4
–1.49 to –1.0	23.9	9.2
–0.99 to –0.5	15.0	15.0
–0.49 to 0	9.7	19.1
0.01 to 0.5	5.5	19.1
0.51 to 1.0	3.5	15.0
1.01 to 1.5	0.0	9.2
1.51 to 2.0	0.0	4.4
2.01 to 2.5	0.0	1.7
2.51 to 3.0	0.0	0.5
3.01 to 3.5	0.0	0.1

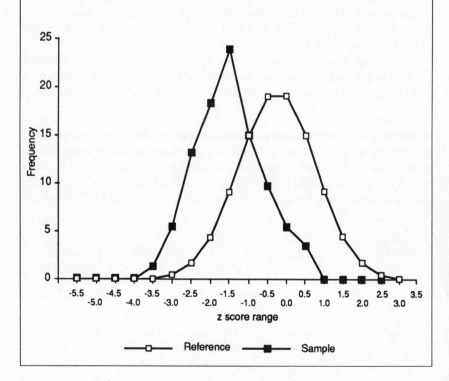

more common between the ages of approximately six months and two years, while the cumulative effects of stunting are rare before two years.

During periods of acute food insecurity and famine, as the prevalence of wasting increases, the distribution of wasting across age groups changes as an increased proportion of older children become wasted (Kloth *et al.*, 1976, Seaman *et al.*, 1978). Wasting under two years of age is partly associated with weaning problems, whereas wasting above two years is more likely to be a result of food shortages and reduced food intake.

Another reason for categorizing anthropometric data is problems with the international reference data (discussed more fully later in this chapter). Irregularities in the reference data exaggerate the prevalence of wasting among children between 12 and 24 months relative to older age groups.

How objective is anthropometric data?

The strong appeal of anthropometric data is because of their objectivity as a precise measure of nutritional status and growth failure. But on closer inspection anthropometric results are not quite as objective as most of us seem to think. To be objective, results must be both valid and reliable.

Box 3.4   Sources of bias in nutrition surveys and surveillance

TYPE OF BIAS	CAUSE
Incomplete coverage	Inaccurate or out-of-date sampling frame. Large-scale population movements; distress migration. Sampling subsections of the population; famine camps, feeding centres.
Clinic bias	Geographical bias towards the more accessible affluent or urban areas. Fluctuating attendance. Selective coverage of the local population. Varying admission criteria.
Age bias	Samples of varying age composition; younger children are more susceptible to wasting, while older children are more susceptible to stunting. All nutritional indices therefore vary according to the age structure of the sample.
Non-random measurement error	Systematic errors because of faulty weighing equipment or incorrect measuring techniques. Inadequate training and supervision. Non-standardized measuring equipment.

Reliability—sources of bias
A reliable measure gives roughly the same answer whenever it is carried out. The design of anthropometric surveys is intended to do just that. Standardized measuring techniques, sampling design and training are all intended to maximize reliability. Statistical checks, such as confidence intervals, provide a measure of the reliability and precision of results. Sample size affects the size of the confidence interval, which widens as sample size decreases.

But a large sample is not enough to guarantee the reliability of results because of the possibility of a biased sample. Various sources of bias common in nutrition surveys are listed in Box 3.4. These may have a profound effect on results, much greater than random measurement errors, which may be removed by the analysis.

Validity—finding the true meaning behind the figures
A measure is valid if it is relevant to the question asked and provides the correct answer. For example, if the question is 'what is the rate of wasting?', a valid measure would be the weight-for-height anthropometric index. Problems with the validity of anthropometric results occur when wide-ranging conclusions are drawn on the basis of anthropometric results alone. This can happen when anthropometry is used as an indirect measure or proxy indicator for some other factor of interest, such as inadequate food intake, or inadequate household food security, etc. Valid conclusions about these factors cannot be drawn from anthropometric data in isolation.

Confounding variables and anthropometric status—watch out for deceptive data
Confounding variables interact with anthropometric indicators and can profoundly affect the reliability and validity of results. For example, high mortality can mask a deteriorating nutritional situation, as can the absence of the most vulnerable members of a community. This type of interaction confuses the true picture and leads to wrong conclusions.

In a deteriorating situation, the death of malnourished children and subsequent raised mortality rates, may mask concurrent changes in anthropometric status. For example, in eastern Sudan the anthropometric status of recently arrived refugees appeared deceptively stable as little change was found in the prevalence of malnutrition over a three-month period. However, this period was marked by food shortages and high incidence of diarrhoea and measles; 13 per cent of children in the camp died. The apparently stable rate of malnutrition was explained by a high mortality amongst malnourished children, who were then replaced by surviving children whose anthropometric status had deteriorated (Nieburg *et al.*, 1988).

Similarly, in Hararghe, Ethiopia, no difference was found between the anthropometric status of nomadic and agricultural groups. However, the death rate amongst children in the nomadic groups was three times the rate found in the agricultural groups (Rivers *et al.*, 1976). Any potential differences between the anthropometric status of these groups may have been masked by the effects of different mortality rates.

Excess mortality among children under five years distorts the age structure of the population. This affects the comparability of results between surveys. If as a result of high mortality the proportion of children under five in the population has fallen, then anthropometric results from this group cannot reliably be compared with a normal population. For example, a survey in Bardera, Somalia in 1993, found that only 3.3 per cent of the total population was under five years (normally around 20 per cent of the population are under five years) as a result of high mortality among this group (Trickett, 1993). This was thought to bias the anthropometric results, which were no longer thought to represent the nutritional situation of the population as a whole. No relation was found between the anthropometric results and food security indicators monitored during the survey (Trickett, 1993).

Movements of large groups of people affect the results of nutrition surveys if the nutritional condition of those who leave is different from those who remain behind, thereby confounding the true anthropometric status of the population.

Limitations of the reference values
One of the great advantages of anthropometric data is that they can be compared with international reference values, and the resulting nutritional indices can then be used to make comparisons between groups, and even between countries. Since 1978 the World Health Organization has adopted the NCHS/CDC reference values as the international growth reference (WHO, 1987). These reference values replace the Harvard (or Boston) standards, which lacked a weight-for-height standard.

The current international reference values are not without their own drawbacks, largely caused by irregularities in the original data. The NCHS/CDC reference growth curves are based on two distinct data sets:

The Fels curves from birth to 3 years. This growth data is from a sample from Yellow Springs, Ohio collected by the Fels Research Institute from 1929 to 1975. Height measurements for this part of the reference were based on recumbent length or supine measurement.
The NCHS curves from 2 to 18 years. This data was taken from three U.S. representative surveys conducted from 1960 to 1975 by the National Center for Health Statistics (NCHS). The height curves for this part of the reference were based on standing measurement (Dibley *et al.*, 1987a, 1987b).

The Fels data are based on length measurements from a localized sample, in contrast to the height measurements of the much larger national NCHS samples.

Because recumbent length is slightly longer than the standing measurement, height measurements are transformed using height reference values from national samples, whereas length measurements are transformed using the Fels curves.

The main problems with these curves are the discontinuities in weight-for-height and height-for-age at the point at which the two data sets overlap (24 months). Over one year of age, weight-for-age is free from significant deviations or inconsistencies.

In the case of weight-for-height there is an abrupt but downward shift in mean Z score at 24 months by approximately 0.4 to 0.5 SD scores. As a result of these irregularities, the prevalence of malnutrition (wasting) among children between 12 and 24 months of age is exaggerated relative to older age groups. This is one reason why anthropometric data should be presented separately for children under and over 24 months.

The irregularities of the reference curves in the charts and tables available from WHO are less than in the original data as the curves have been 'smoothed out'. These growth curves only approximate a normal distribution, so the standard deviations are provided separately for the distributions above and below the median.

Qualitative approaches to gathering information

A wide range of qualitative methods have been developed for collecting data in the context of development projects and surveillance programmes. Several approaches have sprung up in different parts of the world for different purposes. The origins of these methods lie in the qualitative research methods of the social sciences.

Although the names and catch phrases for the different approaches sound confusing, they do in fact have much in common. One of the first applications was rapid rural appraisal (RRA) for farming systems research in the late seventies. RRA was originally intended as an alternative to costly and time-consuming surveys. It was also designed to avoid the biases of 'development tourism'; quick visits by experts that were biased in the people they met and when they occurred. These trips tended to avoid the more difficult travelling conditions of the wet season and as a result failed to visit during the most stressful period of the year (seasonal increases in workload, disease and food shortages).

Rapid assessment procedures (RAP) were originally developed in South America to learn about health-seeking behaviour and views and beliefs about health (Scrimshaw and Hurtado, 1987). This approach has a strong anthropological basis.

Participatory rural appraisal (PRA) has evolved as an outgrowth of RRA, with a shift of emphasis towards full participation and involvement of local people, with outsiders playing a more passive role (Chambers, 1992). Because the objective of PRA is less to gather data and much more to start a participatory process, PRA extends the RRA approach beyond data collection into analysis, planning and action.

Box 3.5   The principles of qualitative methods

Decentralizes gathering of information	RRA is a local activity among a small number of purposively selected communities or households, unlike household surveys which require large samples controlled and managed centrally by outsiders.
Establish a rapport	One of the first aims is to establish a good relationship with local people, respecting their knowledge and abilities.
Flexibility	At any time new lines of enquiry can be explored, existing techniques can be adapted and new ones can be improvised or invented.
Rapid and progressive learning	Learning goes on all the time, and is encouraged by the flexible use of methods and improvisation. There are regular reviews and cross-checkings of findings.
Triangulation	Information is cross-checked and amended by using a range of different methods, and approaching different sources to obtain a more accurate and balanced perspective.
Visualization or mental mapping	The use of visual techniques, such as mapping or scoring, is often revealing and powerful.
Combinations and sequences of methods	These are practical and powerful, for example, a map of the village leads to a discussion about wealth, followed by wealth ranking, routes for a transect walk, etc.
Optimal ignorance	The costs of gathering data are balanced against the value of the information obtained, time is not wasted seeking information that is not needed. Often an approximate picture is more than adequate.
Acknowledges diversity	The narrower focus of RRA leads to greater insights and understanding of local situations, and differences between and within communities and households.
Relative values rather than absolute values	Ranking or scoring give relative values rather than measuring absolute values. This is useful for sensitive information such as income or wealth, as people are often willing to present relative values when they would conceal or distort absolute values.
Multidisciplinary	RRA involves a group of outsiders who bring their individual skills and experience.

Qualitative approaches to gathering information are now much more than an alternative to costly and time-consuming formal surveys; more importantly they provide a different yet invaluable perspective of particular problems. What is often overlooked is that the insights gained from qualitative methods are the ideal complement for the facts and figures of formal surveys. Perhaps the greatest strength of qualitative approaches for those with an interest in nutrition, is their ability to reveal rapidly the underlying causes of malnutrition and show how these are interrelated and might change on a seasonal basis.

Additionally, qualitative methods are appropriate for learning about diversity within the community, or who is malnourished and why. The results of rapid rural appraisal are often more than adequate for the needs of decision makers, but if more detail is required RRA can be used to generate hypotheses to be tested in more formal surveys. For surveillance purposes RRA can be used to identify which quantitative indicators may be worth monitoring.

Qualitative methods differ from quantitative surveys, not just in the techniques that are applied, but also in their basic principles which are summarized in Box 3.5.

Toolbox of techniques—typology of methods

RRA and PRA use a combination of different techniques, which are described in Box 3.6. The list of techniques is forever growing as field-workers improvise, adapt and invent new ones.

Most RRA exercises include at least a review of existing information, direct observation and semi-structured interviewing with groups and individuals. The choice of other techniques depends on the purpose of the assessment.

Instead of random sampling, these techniques purposively select participants according to the points of interest, such as different livelihood systems (farmers, fishermen), or disadvantaged groups, including women. This is one way of offsetting the biases of development tourism.

The strength of RRA lies partly in the power of 'visual sharing'; by creating their own maps, diagrams and matrices, people are better able to describe, explain and discuss complex issues (Chambers, 1992).

Participation as a means of self-reliant development

All qualitative approaches share the principles outlined in Box 3.5. PRA is unique as it takes qualitative methods a significant step further by including the goal of participation in varying degrees. In its fullest sense, participation is a means of empowerment that is directly linked with self-reliant development. Through PRA, people are able to have a say in development activities and take part in the organization and management of activities

Box 3.6 Toolbox of RRA techniques

Use of existing information available from government and agencies in the regional and capital city (reports, articles and papers, government statistics, project documents, maps).

Direct observation of events, relationships and processes.

Semi-structured interviews with focus groups, key informants, purposively selected individuals. A mental or written check-list of key areas or open-ended questions is prepared in advance. Points of interest are followed up.

Do it yourself—local people teach outsiders to perform village tasks.

Participatory mapping and modelling—local people make a map showing those features relevant to them.

Transect walks—a relaxed walk with key informants through an area of interest, which provides an opportunity for observation and discussion.

Timelines—a chronology of events.

Seasonal diagramming—the seasonal pattern of events, such as rainfall, agricultural activities, labour demands, presented visually as a diagram or model.

Wealth ranking—local people rank households according to their perceptions of their wealth status.

Activity profiles and daily routines—people describe their activities for different times of the day, which may be repeated for different seasons.

Matrix scoring and ranking—several similar subjects are ranked or scored according to criteria which are usually decided upon by the people doing the ranking. For example, local preferences for different cereals. The criteria may include: drought resistance, need for fertilizers or other inputs, seasonal availability, labour requirements for production and processing, acceptability, variety of uses, etc. The different cereals would be listed in columns with the criteria in rows.

Pairwise ranking—similar items are compared pair by pair.

Venn diagrams (chapatti diagrams)—local people make their own venn diagrams which identifies the relative importance of local institutions and their interaction with each other.

Stories, portraits and case-studies—illustrative examples.

Shared presentations and feedback sessions—time to share and discuss findings. In PRA local people make presentations.

that will affect them. Empowerment of the rural poor is partly an educational process which builds confidence, and gives people greater independence and control over their own lives.

In contrast, a small degree of participation may simply mean that local people give up some of their time and contribute their skills for particular activities. In this sense, participation of local people is a way of ensuring that other project objectives are met and the project is successful. The outsiders are still very much in charge, while local people have been co-opted to undertake certain tasks.

A successful PRA requires a fundamental change in approach; it is not enough just to adopt a few new techniques. Role reversal and sharing are essential for PRA; local people set the agenda and take the lead in assessing and analysing their situation, while fieldworkers take a back seat and watch, listen and learn.

This usually requires a change in the attitudes, demeanour and behaviour of outsiders, which can be difficult for those of us who hold positions of responsibility and like to think we are authorities in our field. Outsiders act as 'facilitators'; they start the process of PRA, but then allow local people to take the initiative.

Part of the training for a PRA often involves staying or camping in a local village, and learning from villagers how to undertake routine daily tasks. This develops respect for local skills and knowledge and develops critical self-awareness.

Full participation in project activities is needed to ensure the lasting success or 'sustainability' of the project. If local people feel a project is theirs, because they designed it and now manage it, they are more likely to have a vested interest in its success. Projects break down if people are unwilling to support or accept the services offered because their concerns and preferences have been ignored.

Combining qualitative and quantitative methods of gathering information

Qualitative and quantitative methods are often seen as opposites; quantitative data are considered objective and rigorous, while qualitative information is speculative and subjective. These differences do not mean the two approaches are incompatible, although researchers have often favoured one or the other.

In practice, most information gathering, whether it is quantitative or qualitative, includes elements of the other approach. In a formal survey, there are often many examples where a qualitative approach is taken, for example, in interpreting causal relationships, deciphering puzzling responses, presenting case-study illustrations and selecting variables to serve as indices. Likewise qualitative methods may report relevant statistics (secondary data).

Increasingly techniques are being mixed. Sometimes RRA methods use random sampling to select respondents, while questionnaire surveys are increasingly including more open-ended questions and purposive selection of survey sites (Longhurst, 1993). Comparisons of qualitative and quantitative data are encouraging; the relative values generated by ranking and scoring techniques compare favourably with the results of conventional questionnaire surveys (Chambers, 1992).

In practice, these two approaches are complementary as they each make up for the limitations of the other. Quantitative methods are unsuited to causal analysis or understanding the processes of change, while qualitative methods are unable to show the extent or severity of malnutrition (even though they can show malnutrition is present). But if qualitative and quantitative methods are used in combination, it is possible to measure how much or how many, and at the same time give meaning to the facts and figures by explaining who and why. This powerful combination of methods is far superior to the use of either approach in isolation.

All assessments involve an element of judgement on the part of the assessors. The inclusion of qualitative methods provides a toolbox of techniques which help generate the wider and deeper understanding missing from quantitative surveys, which is needed to make sound judgements about complex relationships and the process of change. For nutritional assessments, this means a better understanding of underlying causes of malnutrition and the impact of seasonal change.

Community participation in nutritional surveillance

The reality of community participation has not yet caught up with the rhetoric, or at least the reality recorded in articles, reports and papers. Examples of community-based nutritional surveillance are described in Box 3.7. The goal of full community participation is ideal and the radical changes of approach that are needed are unlikely to be achieved overnight.

There has been a definite shift away from large-scale centrally managed development programmes towards local community-based projects. The days of national nutritional surveys based on grandiose theoretical frameworks followed by a predictable set of technical interventions are, it is hoped, over. Agencies with a major interest in nutrition programmes strongly recommend a participatory approach towards nutrition assessment, analysis and action (UNICEF, 1990). However, these 'bottom-up' processes of empowerment and participation are not a replacement for the necessary 'top-down' planning of national policies. The decision-making processes at different levels of administration should interact and support one another.

Community participation is attractive not just because of its high ideals of empowerment, but also because participatory programmes are more likely to be sustainable long after the first programme managers have left. Initially the start-up costs needed to develop a participatory approach are likely to be high, because of the degree of training required and the input from highly paid specialists. But the development of local human resources and community participation ensures the active support of local people in the long term. As the principles of PRA become more widely practised, the need for outside experts to start the process will decline.

Box 3.7 Examples of community-based nutritional surveillance

The Iringa Nutrition Programme in Tanzania
This was one of the first experiments with the Triple-A approach supported by UNICEF and WHO (JNSP, 1989). Community participation was generated by a vigorous campaign; every village was introduced to the programme and its objectives through talks and motivational films. Local people were trained and all children were weighed and vaccinated (JNSP, 1989). The programme activities resulted in a decrease of severely underweight children (less than 60 per cent weight-for-age of the Harvard standard) from 6.3 per cent during the second quarter of 1982, to 1.8 per cent in the second quarter of 1988.

Nicaragua
Villagers participate in deciding what information to obtain and in designing the data forms. Raw data stay in the village and villagers have begun to formulate community projects based on their own analysis and interpretation of the data (Arnauld *et al.*, 1990).

Zaire
Members of the community collect data on a monthly basis on four indicators: rainfall, market prices, percentage of low-birth-weight babies (<2.5kg) and percentage of pre-school children falling below the lower weight curve (corresponding to the third centile) on the Road to Health Charts. Data are primarily intended for use by the community, but they are also submitted in standard format to higher authorities. Actual examples of the use of the data are not given although three hypothetical cases are described (Brown, 1990).

The Darfur case-study presented in Part 2 describes the evolution of a new approach to nutritional surveillance for the purposes of early warning and targeting. This experimental project purposively selected sentinel sites, and adapted a mix of methods to suit the local circumstances. The new approach evolved from the practical problems of gathering information during the drought years of the mid-eighties.

PART 2

NUTRITION IN ACTION

A case-study of Darfur

CHAPTER 4

Famine in Darfur 1984–5

Introduction

The 1984–5 famine was one of the most severe in the history of Darfur and for the first time, Darfur was the focus of an international famine relief operation. The main focus of famine relief was to provide food aid in the form of relief grain to make up the harvest shortfalls, and to a much lesser extent supplementary foods to counter malnutrition. Between 1984 and 1986 over 170 000 tonnes of imported food aid were distributed.

Nutrition surveys played a key role in providing information to relief agencies and donors, most of whom had only recently come to Darfur and knew next to nothing about the region and its people. Some of these surveys provided invaluable information about food security in Darfur, as well as recording the impact of the famine on anthropometric status. This was a considerable achievement given the huge size of Darfur, the diversity of its people and landscapes, and the difficulties of travelling within the region.[1]

Darfur is only one of seven regions in Sudan,[2] but in size it is equal to Kenya (510 000km^2). The population of Darfur is 3.5 million, one-fifth that of Kenya. About 1.5 million live in North Darfur Province, half of whom are concentrated in the more fertile El Geneina area council in the west of the province. In the north-east, communities are small and scattered and the population density is as low as one to two people per square kilometre.

Apart from its huge size, Darfur is noted for its remote location, more than 1 000km from Khartoum. The region is more or less equidistant from the Red Sea, the Mediterranean and the Gulf of Guinea. Before 1990, the overland journey between Khartoum, and El Fasher, the regional capital of Darfur, took several days in the dry season and was often impossible in the

---

[1] There are barely 220km of paved road in Darfur and three routes under gravel tracks. During the rainy season, travel to many parts of the region is hazardous and unreliable, and the westernmost part, in Geneina area council, is often inaccessible.

[2] The names of the administrative divisions in Darfur have recently changed. Up until 1990, Darfur Region was divided into two provinces: North and South Darfur. Within North Darfur there were five area councils: El Fasher, Umm Keddada, Mellit, Kutum and El Geneina. Each area council was subdivided into rural councils, which were further subdivided into village councils.

rainy season. The single railway link is irregular and inefficient and there are no regular flights. Darfur is further isolated by its poor telecommunications, which are limited to radio contact. Darfurs's remote location, exacerbated by its weak infrastructure, has made it one of the least-developed regions in Sudan.

The first half of this chapter explains why Darfur is vulnerable to famine and describes the effects of the 1984–5 famine. The last part of the chapter describes the response of government, donors and relief agencies, and the role of nutrition surveys in providing information about Darfur and the impact of the famine on anthropometric status.

History of famine in Darfur

Famine in Darfur is not just a twentieth-century phenomenon; its long history can be traced back as far as the great 1752–87 famine (de Waal, 1989a). Since that time famine has been a regular occurence, regardless of the varying political and social systems of different governments.

The worst famine in memory occurred between 1888 and 1892. Darfur experienced a severe famine again in 1913–14 and more recently in 1984–5. These were both triggered by drought. The famines that occurred between the fall of the Darfur Empire in 1874 and Anglo-Egyptian Condominium rule in 1916 were often the result of war or civil unrest. There were many years of famine between 1926 and 1973, but these were less severe and were not thought to have resulted in famine deaths.

People were vulnerable to famine in Darfur during the Condominium government because there was little economic development, so when harvests failed there were few economic alternatives. Following the independence of Sudan in 1956, there were more opportunities for waged labour in Darfur partly as a result of the introduction of groundnut cropping and the extension of the railway as far as Nyala in South Darfur. This economic development probably protected Darfur against the worst effects of the Sahelian famine in 1973, unlike the West African Sahel (de Waal, 1989a).

Why is Darfur vulnerable to famine?

Most famines in Darfur have been triggered by drought caused by a wide range of factors. Darfur was prone to famine in 1984–5 as a result of geographic isolation and poor communications, food insecurity, weakness of the economy and political instability in Sudan as a whole (Buchanan-Smith, 1990).

Mellit Area Council and Umm Keddada Area Council in the north-east of the province are the areas of greatest food insecurity. The tribes living in this area include the Meidob, Zayadia and Berti, who are briefly described in Box 4.1. They each have their traditional homeland or 'dar' which does not always correspond to the administrative boundaries.

64

Within Darfur, food shortages and famine affect people differently, according to their livelihood systems and degree of food security. Usually it is the resource-poor who are the most food insecure and likely to be hit hardest by the effects of famine. These may be households with little or low-quality land, with too few animals or that own few other assets. They also include households living in ecologically marginal areas, like much of north-east Darfur. The great majority of pastoralists are vulnerable to food insecurity as many now have insufficient livestock for subsistence. The rising numbers of female-headed households mean they are a growing vulnerable subgroup.

Ecology

The natural environment of Darfur ranges from arid desert in the north to savannah woodland in the south. Much of the eastern half of Darfur is covered with plains of sandy soils and low sandstone hills, known locally as 'goz'. These are usually dry but are often fertile, and are transformed during the rainy season to provide arable land and pasture. Seasonal water courses, known as 'wadis', create small areas of rich alluvial soils. Exposed basement rock, which is too infertile to be cultivated, provides some forest cover and grazing and browse for animals. The desert zone lies north of the sixteenth parallel.

Rainfall

Most rain falls between July and September, half of which can be in August alone. Annual rainfall varies greatly from year to year, both in the total amount and its distribution throughout the rainy season. In terms of crop production, distribution is more important than total annual rainfall. In the desert zone of North Darfur rainfall is low: on average less than 100mm/year and highly variable. Further south, in the sahelian zone, rainfall averages between 100 and 500mm/year and varies between 25 per cent and 35 per cent from year to year (Swift and Gray, 1989). In any one year rainfall is very localized.

Production systems

Traditional, subsistence-oriented, rainfed agriculture is practised by most of the rural population who account for over 85 per cent of the total population. Farmers cultivate millet on *goz*, and traditionally own small numbers of camels, cattle, sheep and goats. Better-off farmers have access to the richer alluvial soils adjacent to wadis, where a range of fruits and vegetables can be grown.

Crops
Millet is the preferred staple crop, followed by sorghum, both of which are grown by rainfed cultivation on *goz*. Because of the variable rainfall,

farmers plant millet over a large area, and only the fields which receive sufficient rainfall are weeded and tended (Ibrahim, 1984). Millet yields vary from an average of 90kg per hectare on the northern edge of the cultivated area, to 400kg per hectare in the southernmost part of North Darfur. This may be halved in a poor year as a result of low rainfall and pests, and doubled in a good year (Swift and Gray, 1989). Even in a good year deficits in the north are usual but are compensated for by surplus production in west and South Darfur.

People are well adapted to cope with fluctuating food production, for example, households usually aim to store surplus grain produce for at least two years after a good harvest, as a buffer for the anticipated dry years. But these systems have come under increasing pressure in recent decades. Over the last 30 years there has been a declining trend in rainfall, combined with a growing population.

Watermelon is the main intercrop in *goz* areas of North Darfur, although sesame, okra and groundnuts are also grown. Groundnuts are the main cash crop.

Wild foods
In parts of North Darfur, berries, nuts and the seeds of wild grasses and thorns are collected and traditionally supplement the diet, particularly among nomadic and semi-nomadic tribes. Among the Zaghawa people, the management and harvesting of wild seeds was traditionally more important than the cultivation of millet.

Some wild foods are eaten regularly and are even considered a delicacy, for example, 'difra' or wild rice is cooked with milk and sugar. The sweet berries, 'girgedan' and 'gidem' and 'nabak', are often eaten as a snack, especially during Ramadan. Wild seeds are often used to prepare drinks or porridge or added to millet or sorghum to make it go further.

Certain wild foods are less desirable, as they are unpalatable or difficult to collect or prepare and are regarded as distress foods and only eaten

---

Table 4.1   Common wild foods in North Darfur

LOCAL NAME	LATIN NAME
Lalob (fruit)	*Balanites aegyptiaca*
Nabak (sweet berry)	*Zizyphus spina-Christi*
Mukheit (berry)	*Boscia senegaliensis*
Ardaib	*Tamarindus indica*
Direisa (grass seed)	*Tribulus terrestris*
Difra (wild rice)	*Echinochloa colonum*
Girgedan and gidem (berries)	*Grewia* species
Koreb (seed)	*Brachiaria xantholeuca, Dactyloctenium aegyptium*

when other sources of food are under pressure. The mukheit berry (*Boscia senegaliensis*) is the most common distress food used in north-east Darfur.

Distress foods are described in more detail in the next chapter.

Pastoralism

Pastoralism dominates in the north of the province among the Meidob, Zayadiya and Zawghawa tribes. Camels, sheep and goats are kept, and in the past cows were also owned.

Box 4.1   Tribes in north-east Darfur

The Meidob
Traditionally, the Meidob herd sheep and camels in a completely mobile manner, whereas cattle and goats are kept near the settlement. An assured supply of drinking-water and permanent pasture in the Meidob hills meant that the Meidob did not have to leave their homeland to find water and pasture for their livestock. During the 1970s the Meidob population and livestock numbers expanded, but there was little emigration. Grazing capacity became restricted and the pressure on remaining pasture areas increased. Many trees died. The Meidob grow some millet, although production is highly erratic. Even in years of highest rainfall, the grain produced is not sufficient to cover subsistence needs.

Overall, the Meidob were less affected by the drought in the 1970s than neighbouring tribes. As a result they were not forced to diversify their means of subsistence or establish bases elsewhere in Darfur. This meant they were all the more vulnerable to the effects of the 1984–5 famine.

The Zayadiya
The homeland of the Zayadiya arabs is in the south-east of Mellit Area Council and extends approximately 450km in a north–south direction. The Zayadiya are nomads in the process of becoming settled (Ibrahim, 1984). The northern Zayadiya remain camel-herding nomads with pasture areas, while those in the south have become settled millet farmers. In the transitional stage, women grow millet and the men migrate from the homeland with their animals in search of pasture.

Traditionally, with the first rains, the Zayadiya take their camels and sheep to South Darfur until August, after which they migrate northwards to the pasture around Mareiga. They return to their village in September. In very wet years, the winter months are spent as far as 500km to the north-west, in the Jizu areas near Wadi Howar (Ibrahim, 1984).

The Berti
The Berti homeland extends from the Berti Hills in Mellit Area Council to the eastern border of Umm Keddada (Ibrahim, 1984). The Berti are settled *goz* farmers, cultivating mostly millet. Prior to the drought years of the 1970s the Berti regularly produced a surplus of millet and many also had a source of income from gum arabic. As a result of the drought, virtually all the gum arabic trees (Acacia senegal) died, and millet production fell despite extensive cultivation. Subsequently, the main source of income was the sale of livestock. Herds were restructured: goats increased in numbers as numbers of cows and sheep declined.

Pastoralists are vulnerable to shifts in the grain/livestock terms of trade. Drought followed by a poor harvest causes grain prices to rise and livestock prices to fall as a result of increased sales, which is to the disadvantage of pastoralists and farmers whose assets are held in livestock.

Markets

Rich and poor, farmers and pastoralists, participate in the market, both for purchasing foods and disposing of surplus production and assets. In good years the grain market works relatively well within Darfur, but its geographic isolation means that it is not well integrated into the national grain marketing network. The market cannot be relied upon to import grain into the region in substantial amounts. As a result, inadequate grain production in Darfur can rapidly become a serious regional food shortage (Buchanan-Smith, 1990). In poor years, supplies to remote northern markets quickly dry up because of costly and difficult transport, particularly during the rainy season when market supplies are most needed (Buchanan-Smith and Mohammed, 19?).

Livestock markets provide a collection system for the supply of meat to the towns, and for the export of animals. Most livestock exports are direct, on foot, from the region. Camels are exported to Egypt and Libya, and cows to Central African Republic, or to Omdurman (Swift and Gray, 1989).

Trade in other commodities from Central Sudan is also affected by the weak infrastructure and remote location. For example, sugar sold in Darfur is often more than five times the price in Central Sudan (when it is available at all in Darfur). The cost of living is inevitably higher in Darfur than in the rest of the country.

Drought culminates in famine, 1984–5

Darfur experienced several drought years in the early eighties, which triggered the 1984–5 famine. The famine started in the north-east of Darfur, which suffered partial crop failure in 1982, and was followed by almost complete crop failure in 1983. Finally, in 1984 the harvest failed for the majority of farmers throughout North Darfur (Ibrahim, 1990). At the same time there was harvest failure throughout Sudan and in neighbouring countries, which exacerbated problems in Darfur.

Crop production figures reported by the Regional Ministry of Agriculture show the decreasing production in Darfur: from 362 000 metric tonnes in 1982–3, to 237 000 tonnes in 1983, to a rough estimate for 1984 of less than 200 000 tonnes (Pearson, 1986).

According to de Waal, after the harvest failure of 1984 people began to eat fewer, smaller and less pleasant meals. They ate less millet and sorghum and more wild foods. Some had already been doing this for some time, after the failure of the harvest of 1983 in North Darfur.

The famine was not a general phenomenon, nor did it affect all areas with equal severity. It was particularly severe where it had started in the north-east in parts of Mellit and Umm Keddada. In the west of Darfur on the border with Chad, the presence of large numbers of recently arrived Chadian refugees triggered a serious localized crisis.

After several drought years, the rains in 1985 were good and most people who had left their farms during the famine returned to plant their crops. There were widespread shortages of seed, but still thousands cultivated whatever they could, including in some cases, relief sorghum. Crop production in 1985 was still low, with those areas that had been most affected by famine having again the lowest production (Ibrahim, 1990). Even so the rains of 1985 signalled the start of the recovery.

Loss of livestock

Huge numbers of livestock were sold before the livestock market collapsed, or died for lack of water and pasture. Pastoralists living in the north of Darfur suffered particularly heavy losses, although many farmers also owned livestock as a form of insurance and were severely affected. Apart from heavy losses, herds were restructured in favour of the more drought-resistant livestock. Cattle were the least drought-resistant animals and the loss percentage in North Darfur in 1984–5 were estimated at 71 per cent compared with 40 per cent goat losses, 24 per cent sheep losses and only 5 per cent camel losses.

In September 1984, a sheep or goat sold for three Sudanese pounds, while a 90kg sack of sorghum cost over 200 Sudanese pounds.[3] By the end of 1984 the nomadic economy throughout north Sudan had collapsed as a result of the worsening terms of trade.

The Meidob were among the worst-affected people in the region. Their sheep and goat herds were approximately halved and cows were reduced to less than a tenth of their original number. Loss of camels was much lower. Tree stocks were also decimated during the famine.

Livestock migration patterns changed as a result of the famine. Among the Meidob those with mobile herds (camel and sheep) now migrate further south, often to Umm Keddada, but sometimes as far as South Darfur. In very dry years livestock may not return to Dar Meidob at all.

Coping strategies

The success of different households in coping with famine varied according to their income and assets and also their participation in community networks of risk-sharing and support.

---

[3] A family of five would consume about one 90kg sack per month in normal times.

The Berti were vulnerable to the effects of drought in the seventies and consequently their way of life had already undergone a transformation. By 1984–5 they were more effective at securing outside assistance than many of the other tribes in Darfur, and Berti villages were among the first to have established feeding centres (de Waal, 1989).

The Meidob were not as badly affected by drought in the seventies as their neighbouring tribes. When the 1984–5 famine struck, their livelihoods were still very much based on livestock, which meant they had few alternative opportunities for earning income. Also they did not have established bases elsewhere in Darfur (Mollison, 1986). Since at that time many more adult men migrate outside of Dar Meidob in search of work.

Water

Water supplies are critical to the survival of livestock and people. During the dry season of 1984–5 many hand-dug wells ran dry, and villages were abandoned (de Waal, 1989). Payments for water were high and could account for up to two-thirds loss of family cash income (Shepherd, 1991).

Migration

Migration was also a widespread phenomenon in the early eighties as adult men travelled increasingly to find work, and people migrated from the more arid North Darfur to the more fertile South Darfur. By 1984 entire families were on the move as people were forced by destitution to migrate from their homes. By May 1985 it was estimated that 300 000 people were living in camps around urban areas (this included 100 000 Chadians). Oxfam estimated that there were more than 1 million internally displaced persons, most of whom were living in scattered groups rather than larger camps (Winer, 1985). Between 300 000 and 500 000 people from Darfur were thought to have moved to Central Region of Sudan and Khartoum (Pearson, 1986). But other estimates are much more conservative, and suggest that numbers migrating from Darfur to central Sudan during the famine period were no more than migration in previous years (de Waal, 1989). Even though the order of magnitude of these estimates vary, there is little doubt that distress migration was a widespread occurrence in late 1984 and continued into 1985.

The patterns of migration varied for different tribes. Some members of the Zawghawa, whose homeland is the north-west of Darfur, moved as far as South Darfur and settled with relatives; others moved to the towns of El Fasher, Nyala, Zalingei and Mellit.

The Zayadiya migrated as far as Ed Daien in South Darfur, or even further to Bahr el Arab, which is the border with South Sudan and 500km south of their homeland.

The Berti have a long history of migration from their homeland; the largest movements occurred during the famines of 1888–92, and 1913–14.

70

The Berti who moved away have not kept their political links with the northern Berti (de Waal, 1989).

Famine camps

As the destitute gathered on the outskirts of towns, camps of displaced people began to form. In North Darfur, camps were established in El Fasher, Mellit and Malha, and in South Darfur, there were camps near Nyala, and in Buram. The population of Malha increased fourfold from 2 000 to 8 000 because of the arrival of drought-affected Meidob. After the famine, many of the poor and destitute remained in Malha.

Mawashei camp, situated on the western side of El Fasher, existed before the famine. By mid-1985 the number of migrants in the camp had increased to 5 000, although there were perhaps 25 000 famine migrants living in El Fasher as a whole (de Waal, 1989).

Famine deaths

Estimates of famine deaths vary greatly, according to Adams and Hawksley (1987); between 50 000 and 150 000 people died in Darfur as a direct result of the famine.

A demographic survey was undertaken in eight villages between April and July, 1986 (de Waal, 1989). Despite the problems of selecting a suitable baseline for comparing mortality, and the difficulties of eliminating biases, the survey indicates that mortality was over three times the normal.

Excess mortality was closely related to age. Child mortality (one to four years) rose sharply (sixfold) relative to both adult and infant mortality (threefold). De Waal attributes the higher child mortality to weaning late (frequently after 18 months) and no bottle feeding. Mortality was higher for males than females in most age groups over five years.[4]

The crude death rate averaged 28.2 per 1 000 for the two years from June 1984 to June 1986. Most excess deaths occurred during the dry season and the rains of 1985; from January 1985 the rate was 40.2. From this, figures for excess deaths are estimated for 1985 to be 85 500 (for 1984–6 to be 95 000). De Waal revises these figures on the basis of an estimated under-reporting of infant mortality by 30 per cent: the CDR rises to 42.6 and the total excess mortality for 1984–6 rises to 107 800.

There was a 'lag' in mortality; 'its rise and fall lagged behind indicators of destitution and food consumption (and child malnutrition)' (de Waal, 1989).

---

[4] The age and sex structure of the population was strikingly unusual. The small cohort of children less than five years old was due to lower fertility and higher mortality. Out-migration of men contributed to an unbalanced sex ratio—93.5 overall, and 66.9 for ages 20–39 (de Waal, 1989b).

The most frequently mentioned cause of death was diarrhoea. In drought-stricken Darfur, water-borne diarrhoea was a disease of both the dry and the wet seasons. During the dry season, wells ran dry or were short of water, and bacterial concentration was likely to increase. During the rains, pollutants were washed into the wells, and population concentrations put pressure on water and sanitation facilities. Measles, which is a dry-season disease, was more common than malaria which is a wet-season disease. Other causes of death included the increase in violence associated with social disruption, and food poisoning from eating improperly prepared wild foods (de Waal, 1989b).

Institutional response to the 1984–5 famine

Government response

As early as October 1983, the governor of Darfur appealed for drought assistance to central government but got no response. The governors of both western and eastern regions of Sudan made further requests in early 1984. The Darfur regional government was supplying some grain but needed more.

The slow and inadequate response of central government prompted the governor of Darfur to resign in April 1984. This protest caused a public outcry, which finally brought into focus the severity of the drought (Pearson, 1986).

The central government banned sorghum exports in March, 1984 and increased the area under sorghum cultivation in the irrigated areas of central Sudan. During April and May, 5 400 tonnes of sorghum were sent by the government to Darfur (Pearson, 1986).

In early June President Nimeiri visited Darfur in response to criticism of central government's lack of interest in the problems there, and on 31 July he declared a state of emergency. By early August the government had arranged the supply of more grain to the west—13 500 tonnes of sorghum to Darfur (35 per cent was to be distributed free, 15 per cent sold at 60 per cent of cost price and 50 per cent sold at cost price). The central government in Khartoum also set up a relief committee for Darfur, however, 'the committee was never very successful as it was not a priority of the chairman' (Pearson, 1986).

Nimeiri refused to publicize the impending famine and it was not until after he was ousted in the April 1985 coup that aid agencies had the freedom to move into relief work in Darfur (Adams and Hawksley, 1989).

Over 100 agencies arrived in Sudan in the first six months of 1985; in Darfur there was 'a proliferation of agencies—multilateral and bilateral, large and small, government and non government, many of them entering the area for the first time and each with their own logistical and support problems'(Adams and Hawksley, 1989). Relief activity gathered momentum and peaked in May and 1985—many months after the first appeals by the regional governors for emergency support.

Several factors hampered and delayed the response, including the lack of a permanent institution responsible for famine preparedness and co-ordination of a response, the absence of a famine policy and the slow official recognition of the risky situation (Teklu *et al.*, 1991). The development of the 1984–6 famine in Sudan and the institutional response has been described in detail by Pearson (1986).

Assessment of relief grain needs and response by donors

Many international missions visited western Sudan to make their own assessments of the situation and estimate the need for relief grain. In late January, 1984, FAO in Khartoum sent a three-day fact-finding mission to Darfur and Kordofan, which led to a request to FAO in Rome for 93 600 tonnes of food aid. This met with some scepticism so Rome sent another mission to review the request. They concluded there was currently no crisis, and in addition the government did not have the capacity to transport the food which had been requested. The previous request was revised downwards to 12 000 tonnes of grain, 7 000 tonnes of which was for Darfur (Pearson, 1986).

During April and June USAID undertook missions to western Sudan and concluded, as FAO had done in January, that the west needed emergency food aid. In September 1984, USAID approved 82 000 tonnes of relief grain for western Sudan and then a further 250 000 tonnes in late 1984 and early 1985, half of which was intended for Darfur (Keen, 1991). A request was also made to increase Sudan's allocation of Title 1 wheat from 250 000 tonnes to 396 000 tonnes. Thus a total of 738 338 tonnes of food aid was being called for by USAID, which in retrospect was thought to be 'a considerable overestimation of need' (Pearson, 1986).

In August 1984, a multi-donor UN mission (UNDP, FAO, WFP and UNICEF) together with the regional governments estimated how many people were affected or seriously affected, and calculated tonnages of emergency food.

A further WFP/FAO multi-donor mission in early 1985 estimated grain deficits of 335 000 tonnes for Darfur, which were considerably greater than the WFP estimates of a deficit of 238 000 tonnes issued in November 1984 (Pearson, 1986).

Emergency relief efforts became fragmented as different donors made their own assessments and individual plans for securing food aid and implementing a response. Relations between leading agencies were sometimes acrimonious (Pearson, 1986).

Distribution and targeting of food aid

From the beginning of the relief operation, targeting was a sensitive political issue. Food aid was originally provided by USAID on the assumption that it would be targeted at those most in need of assistance. This contrasted with the view of the Darfur government which considered general distribution to the entire population to be a fair and just method of allocation because everyone had suffered losses from the drought. Initially food aid was not officially targeted at areas with the most urgent requirements (Buckley, 1988).

By mid-1985 it was mutually agreed between local government and the agencies that relief grain was to be targeted at the neediest one-third of the population (Keen, 1991; Buckley, 1988).

Save the Children Fund (SCF) was the main agency distributing food aid. During 1986 they distributed 46 000 tonnes of USAID and EEC sorghum in North Darfur. SCF established a food information system to assist with the targeting of food aid. The food information system had two components: a monthly household survey, coupled with a network of field officers who collected more qualitative information. Darfur region was divided into 10 assessment zones. From each zone, 40 village councils were selected at random. Monthly socio-economic surveys were carried out by 14 teams.

In practice, allocations of relief grain were made largely on the basis of the field officers' assessments of need and their recommendations, rather than the survey data from the household survey. Responses to the household questionnaires were sometimes felt by the SCF field officers to be prejudiced by the knowledge that SCF was distributing food aid. The data were used to calculate the degree of 'sustainability' and hence deficit in percentage terms (Buckley, 1988). As well as an assessment of need, accurate population estimates were also needed to ensure fair and just allocations, but these were notoriously difficult to ascertain.

Despite the declared intention of targeting the most needy, Keen (1991) found that relief food was not successfully targeted, but instead was spread over very large numbers of recipients throughout the region with little regard for need. He reports the failure of targeting by area councils; people in bigger towns received more relief grain than those in the smaller towns, and townspeople received more than villagers. Migrants on the edges of towns were repeatedly discriminated against, and nomads also got less than their fair share. Within villages, blanket distribution was favoured, but it was generally difficult or impossible for the poor to stake a preferential claim.

Supplementary feeding programmes

The Sudanese Red Crescent (SRC)in conjunction with the the League of Red Cross Societies (LRCS), automatically distributed lentils and oil to all households in those villages where more than 25 per cent of children were acutely malnourished (less than 80 per cent weight-for-height). This was intended to supplement the grain distributed by SCF. Where the malnutrition rate was between 10 per cent and 25 per cent, the SRC/LRCS would sometimes distribute oil and lentils to a limited number of families selected by the village sheikh or the SRC representatives.

The EEC funded three agencies to undertake selective feeding programmes in Darfur. Médecins Sans Frontières–Holland (MSF) organized selective feeding centres for children in those villages in north Darfur where the prevalence of acute malnutrition was greater than 15 per cent. These centres were small, on average only about 20 children were registered (Pearson, 1986). By March 1986, MSF were operating 261 centres and still opening new ones. By May 1986 they decided to close all centres because they found little or no improvement in nutritional status among attending children and also attendance was poor. MSF then radically changed the direction of their programme and proceeded on a path of rehabilitation of the health-service infrastructure.

In South Darfur, MSF Belgium took a similar approach to MSF–Holland in the north. In the refugee camps in west Darfur GOAL organized selective feeding programmes and public health.

Emergency public health measures

The institutional response to the famine was primarily concerned with emergency food aid, while public health interventions received far less attention and fewer resources. In 1984 coverage of measles immunization was extremely poor. There had been no programme to vaccinate children for at least three years in many areas of Darfur and so most children were unprotected. There were measles vaccines in Sudan, provided by UNICEF for the national immunization campaign, although these were not immediately available for emergency immunization programmes (Pearson, 1986). A parallel operation for importing vaccines from Europe was set up by UNHCR, with the assistance of Oxfam, SCF and MSF–France. The system was 'chaotic, time consuming and expensive'. By the time the system was streamlined, there had been hundreds of measles-related deaths (Pearson, 1986). Supplies of essential drugs were equally inadequate although the supplementary feeding programmes organized by MSF–Holland, MSF–Belgium and GOAL included a health component and provided health workers with essential drug kits.

Water programmes were rare, apart from Oxfam's work in ensuring an adequate water supply in the refugee camps and neighbouring settlements.

Role of nutrition information—from shortage to excess

The various missions came up with wildly conflicting opinions about the scale of the emergency aid needed. These differences were partly attributed to a lack of technical expertise and ignorance of the country

(Pearson, 1986). The scale of the planned operation[5] was largely determined by the impact of foreign journalists, and the amount of exposure given to foreign diplomats and representatives of NGOs. But often it was the results of nutritional assessments that gave the NGOs the vital information to feed the media and back the claim that Darfur was in the grip of a nutritional crisis.

Most agencies arriving in Darfur in early 1985 were working in an information vacuum. They were new to the area, and wanted to make immediate decisions about where to work and what to do and to persuade others they were doing the right thing. Anthropometric surveys were the best available option for gathering relevant information, as they would provide apparently objective data directly related to the severity and extent of the nutritional crisis.

In common with the wider response, the initial efforts to undertake nutrition surveys were uncoordinated, and too often surveys were undertaken by unqualified people and the reports often interpreted by managers to suit their own priorities (Pearson, 1986).

Between 1985 and 1986 region-wide nutrition (anthropometric) surveys of Darfur and Kordofan were undertaken jointly by Oxfam, the Ministry of Health and UNICEF under the banner of the Nutritional Surveillance and Drought Monitoring Programme (NSDMP). At the same time several individual NGOs undertook numerous smaller nutrition surveys of particular villages or camps. These activities are described below.

In January 1986 the NSDMP organized a workshop intended to standardize anthropometric survey methods used by the various agencies in Darfur. Several agencies working elsewhere in Sudan participated in this workshop and adopted many of the agreed procedures.

The Sudanese Red Crescent

The Sudanese Red Crescent with assistance from the League of Red Cross Societies had four mobile nutrition survey teams stationed in El Fasher, Kebkabiya, Mellit and Umm Keddada. Each team was headed by League nurses. Village councils that were reportedly 'hardest hit' were purposively selected. The teams used a 'Nabarro' weight-for-height chart to measure anthropometric status and assess the prevalence of wasting. Additional information was collected about the health and socio-economic situation. During the relief operation these teams measured over 44 000 children.

---

[5] In practice, the scale of the operation was far smaller than originally intended as it was severely limited by logistical setbacks, in particular, difficulties of bringing food into Sudan, transporting it to Darfur and then on to the final distribution points within Darfur. An Oxfam survey reported that 'tiny amounts of food aid have reached village people so far'; overall the average amount of sorghum per person was 14g compared with a target of 500g per person per day (Taylor, 1985).

The Nutritional Surveillance and Drought Monitoring Programme (NSDMP)

In September 1984 the Oxfam representative in Khartoum and a representative of UNICEF visited Kordofan and in co-operation with the regional government undertook a rapid survey of nutritional status. During this short visit they measured the mid-upper arm circumference of 1 890 children from 21 sites in North and South Kordofan and found 49 per cent to be malnourished (MUAC less than 13.5cm) (Winer and Zins, 1984).

Prompted by what they had seen, in early 1985, they jointly established the NSDMP, which was intended to provide information to government and potential donors about the needs for food aid, and to assist with the targeting and monitoring of aid (Taylor, 1985). Oxfam provided two nutritionists to co-ordinate survey activities and give technical support. These nutritionists designed and implemented several rounds of region-wide nutrition surveys. The Ministry of Health seconded personnel for the teams and UNICEF presumably provided the vehicles and other essential costs.

Three cycles of region-wide surveys were undertaken in Darfur based on a two-stage cluster design (Taylor, 1985; Williams, 1986) which was typical of the standard nutrition survey cluster design described in Chapter 3. These surveys were dominated by technical considerations of how best to obtain reliable estimates of the prevalence of malnutrition.

The surveys' reports also provided a wealth of qualitative information as a result of extensive field-work that took the teams across the length and breadth of Darfur. They provided detailed background information about food security in Darfur before and during the famine, and gave some indication of which areas were most affected. They also reported the considerable delays in providing food assistance, and recommended prioritizing the delivery of relief food to displaced people, the rural poor and the urban poor.

Although quantitative assessments of anthropometric status dominated these surveys, there is no doubt that qualitative methods of direct observation and informal discussion played a key role. Certainly, the conclusions and recommendations were largely based on qualitative judgements of need.

The NSDMP ceased suddenly in 1986 when the Darfur and Kordofan regional Ministries of Health switched their attention from the regional surveys to the first 'national' nutrition survey—The Sudan Emergency and Recovery Information and Surveillance System (SERISS) in north Sudan.

Use of nutrition data, 1984–6

The flurry of survey activity between 1984 and 1986 produced a wealth of information about the nutrition and food security of the people of Darfur. Nutritional assessments played an important role in keeping donors and agencies informed. According to Pearson (1986), the NSDMP survey reports, 'provided precious information for an area about which little up-to-date information was available. The detail was particularly interesting to administrators away from the action, such as the AID people behind desks in Washington, who were nevertheless involved in the making of important decisions regarding the emergency operation.'

Apart from providing outsiders with 'interesting' information about Darfur, the results of nutritional surveys were principally used for the purposes of advocacy, targeting the distribution of relief grain and supplementary feeding programmes.

Advocacy

The results of nutritional surveys were needed to make assessments of the situation sound more objective and therefore justify the need for aid. Most of the NGOs were active in publicizing the scale of the developing crisis in sub-Saharan Africa. Rates of malnutrition were centre stage in the agencies' efforts to lobby the press and encourage journalists to record what was happening in Africa.

There were no co-ordinated information systems or channels and so the agencies relied on their own informal channels for disseminating the results of surveys. Most NGOs had a direct line of communication with the key multilateral and bilateral donors as well as various government departments. Anthropometric results continued to be centre stage even when contradictory results were presented and agencies began to argue about the technical validity of different approaches.

Not everybody was at ease with the anthropometric yardstick for the assessment of food shortage and famine. The Oxfam representative in Juba, south Sudan, expressed 'extreme concern that a simple and often unreliable anthropometric system of nutrition status assessment should have become the predominant, if not the sole criterion, for food intervention among the major donors' (Stockton, 1986).

Targeting relief grain, 1985 and 1986

Two agencies used a cut-off level of malnutrition to target supplementary feeding programmes. MSF–Holland considered this to be politically sensitive and easy to apply. The LRCS nutritionist at that time thought too much emphasis was put on anthropometry alone but she acknowledged that rates of malnutrition were convenient to refer to when pressure was applied by 'non-needy villages' (Lowgren, 1986).

Anthropometric data were not used in isolation to target relief grain at specific areas, although the network of SCF field officers frequently referred to anthropometric data to justify their arguments for ending distribution of relief grain (Buckley, 1988). According to one field officer, the 'quasi-neutrality of hard quantitative data' was of value in making targeting decisions that were politically unpopular (Mollison, 1986).

Lessons from Darfur for future nutrition surveys

Many difficulties were encountered during the survey activities of 1984–6. Some were a result of using sampling techniques unsuited to a famine situation in an area as large and diverse as Darfur. The many other problems were common to nutrition surveys throughout the Sahel at that time. For example, slow turnaround of information, weak or limited interpretation of underlying causes and high costs contributing to poor sustainability. Box 5.1 in the next chapter describes these problems more fully and presents solutions.

The experience of nutrition surveys in Darfur and elsewhere during the famine years of the mid-eighties served as important lessons for future surveillance activities. The next chapter describes events in Darfur in the years following the famine. An early warning system was established, part of which was a community-based nutritional surveillance programme.

CHAPTER 5
After the famine—a shift in approach

Introduction

In 1986, the rains were good for the second year running and most farmers in Darfur produced a surplus. By now the 1984–5 famine relief operation was in full swing, albeit too late. Plans were set in motion to phase out relief distribution of food, and the transition from relief to recovery began in earnest. The agencies which remained after the famine emergency changed direction from top-down relief programmes to more community-based development activities, most of which were either in the health sector or small-scale water supply and agriculture.

In 1986 the Agricultural Planning Unit (APU) was established in El Fasher in an attempt to involve the regional government in planning the post-drought recovery and co-ordinating the activities of agencies and government departments. This was a significant change from the previous famine relief efforts, which were largely centralized and implemented by outside agencies.

Famine preparedness was uppermost in the objectives of the APU. They established a regional information system, one role of which was famine early warning. Very soon after its commencement, the APU was predicting widespread harvest failure as a result of the poor rains of 1987.

Donors and government were in a responsive mood as they were concerned that there would be a rapid deterioration as the harvest failure followed so soon after the catastrophic famine of 1984–5. Even before the harvest assessment was completed in February 1988, donors had committed resources to the region and the 'Western relief operation' was planned.

The Western relief operation aimed to deliver grain to areas affected by harvest failure and to strengthen local government institutions. This was a much smaller operation than the 1984–6 famine relief, but unfortunately, the operation was unsuccessful on both counts. Only a fraction of the planned relief grain was delivered to Darfur, and what did arrive was very late.[1] The

---

1 Only 14 400 tonnes of the agreed 51 000 tonnes of relief needs reached Darfur. There were delays in the release of grain from the Agricultural Bank of Sudan, and in the organization of transport to Darfur (Buchanan-Smith, 1989). The regional relief committee in Darfur had inadequate staff and resources, and staff at lower administrative levels had a limited understanding of how relief needs should be calculated and distributed according to need. Allocations were usually made according to population. At a local level, 85 per cent of the relief grain was sold at subsidized rates through the local government's sugar co-operatives. The remaining 15 per cent was intended for free distribution to the poorest people by the Sudanese Red Crescent. Targeting the poor met with considerable local resistance and consequently a large proportion of people received very small amounts of free grain.

operation highlighted the weaknesses of local institutions, but there had been barely any back-up support or prior training (Buchanan-Smith, 1989). The western relief operation consequently had very little impact.

This chapter describes the development of the early warning system in Darfur, an important part of which was community-based nutritional surveillance. This programme took innovative new approaches to gathering information, and was based on a mix of methods that evolved from the experiences of nutritional surveys throughout the Sahel in 1984–6. The early warning system provided an in-depth picture of nutrition and food security. This is described in the last part of the chapter, and includes some surprising discoveries about nutrition, wealth and food security.

The development of an early warning system in Darfur: 1987–90

Following the famine, there were significant changes in approach; co-operation and collaboration between agencies and with local government improved greatly, and all levels of local government were expected to play a much greater role in famine preparedness and response. The monitoring system of the APU was the result of the co-ordinated efforts of a number of government institutions, development projects and NGOs, including the drought-monitoring programme of the Sudanese Red Crescent (SRC), and Oxfam's nutritional surveillance programme. This co-operation and collaboration was essential for enriching the depth and breadth of coverage of the system and contrasts with the independent and uncoordinated information systems used during the famine.

The information system of the APU covered all of Darfur, while the early warning component focused its attention on North Darfur, which is more prone to drought and food insecurity. The early warning system took a food security oriented approach to monitoring the development of famine and was based on low-cost and innovative methods. The Overseas Development Administration (ODA) provided funding and technical assistance to the APU until 1991.

The APU organized annual harvest assessments and regular monitoring of rainfall and market conditions (prices, availability, trading conditions). Other important sources of information contributing to the early warning system were the drought-monitoring programme of the Sudanese Red Crescent and the nutritional surveillance programme organized by Oxfam.

The APU published a quarterly bulletin which presented the results of the various monitoring activities, including analyses of the food security situation, and recommendations for action. The bulletin served two purposes: its main aim was to function as an aid for regional government for general food security and agricultural planning, but information was also presented to meet the needs of donors and inform national government about Darfur.

The bulletin had wide circulation within Darfur, in Khartoum and even internationally. The predictions and recommendations were fed into the national EWS, but there was no formal institutional link between information and response. Specific action in response to the recommendations made by the bulletin was never guaranteed. Darfur itself had very few resources to launch its own response and had to depend on Khartoum and donor agencies (Buchanan-Smith *et al.*, 1991).

Elements of the early warning system in Darfur

Pre-harvest assessments
Food security assessments in October, just prior to the harvest, were used to estimate cereal production and the possible need for relief. These assessments were the main component of the early warning system. Apart from crop forecasts, the assessments surveyed pas*··re conditions, grain and livestock prices, terms of trade, other income sources, unusual migrations and collection of wild foods. The APU was responsible for overall planning, co-ordination, analyses and report writing, while several agencies participated in the field-work and analyses. Rapid Rural Appraisal techniques were used for data collection.[2]

Market and rainfall monitoring
The APU established a market-monitoring network, and also a rainfall-monitoring system. Prices for grain and livestock were collected three times a month in at least 13 markets throughout North Darfur. For all markets, a monthly average was calculated for each commodity, as well as the monthly livestock/grain terms of trade. Rainfall was monitored in about 25 rainfall stations throughout Darfur.

The drought-monitoring programme of the Sudanese Red Crescent
This programme was started as a pilot project in April 1985, but was temporarily suspended soon after due to the pressure of relief activities. Since 1986, it has been functioning more or less continuously. Nineteen branches of the Sudanese Red Crescent in North Darfur participated in 1988, and provided fairly good geographical coverage. Every month the SRC village drought-monitoring committees completed a questionnaire on the local food security situation. These were then summarized by the drought-monitoring co-ordinator in El Fasher for wider circulation (Borton and Shoham, 1989).

---

[2] In 1988 and 1989, the surveys were based on interviews with key informants in villages purposively selected to give a good representation of the range of villages in North Darfur. After the assessment, districts were categorized according to their food security situation: surplus, self-sufficient, deficit but with other resources, or deficit and resource poor.

The programme has been praised for the use of participatory methods of gathering information within an indigenous NGO, and excellent outreach, low operating costs, and long-term sustainability (Borton and Shoham, 1989). In 1990 the activities of the programme declined because of a combination of problems, including reduced funding, the resignation of the co-ordinator and lack of support to local SRC branches.

The Oxfam nutritional surveillance programme
Oxfam started nutritional surveillance in North Darfur in April 1988, following an invitation from the APU in El Fasher and the Relief and Rehabilitation Commission in Khartoum. The rapid nutrition assessments provided local information which complemented the broader indicators already monitored by the APU. These included information about livelihoods, coping strategies, health and health services and the quality of the diet. This information was relevant in assessing the impact of the failed 1987 harvest on food security and nutrition. The results confirmed the harvest survey reports and described in greater detail the impact of failed harvests on the local communities.

Rapid nutrition assessments continued throughout 1989 and 1990. Longitudinal anthropometric monitoring was established in 1989 in Malha, Mareiga and Cuma, which had not fully recovered from the effects of the 1984–5 famine and were prone to severe seasonal food insecurity. They were expected to show the first signs of additional stress on food security and so provide early warning of deteriorating conditions.

Developments after 1989

The military *coup d'état* in June 1989, which brought an Islamic fundamentalist government to power, seriously affected the ability of the Darfur EWS to elicit a response from either regional or national government, or donors.

The APU's advisory role to the new regional government was not altogether clear. By the end of 1990, the new government established a separate regional planning unit. This included a subcommittee responsible for bringing together information on the food security situation in the region in order to advise on relief and development, which to some extent duplicated the role of the APU.

In September 1990 the expatriate staff were evacuated for security reasons (a feared Chadian invasion), never to return. The same year the ODA withdrew all development aid to Sudan, which included funding for the APU. The Sudanese staff conducted the last pre-harvest survey in October and valiantly attempted to continue work in 1991 in the face of diminishing funding and lack of support. However, the co-operation and collaboration between NGOs working in Darfur, originally encouraged by the APU, remained strong.

By the end of 1991 the Oxfam nutritional surveillance programme was the only part of the regional food information system that still functioned.

New approaches to nutritional surveillance

In 1988 the NGOs were rather reluctant to get embroiled in nutrition surveys again. Once bitten, twice shy; the experiences of 1984 and 1985 had proved costly and not always the success they were intended to be. Information was often was available too late or it was too general to be of any practical use to planners. Nutritionists were often distracted by arguments between themselves over technical details, and had little time to consider new or innovative solutions to the nutritional crisis or to develop a more community-based approach. Well aware of these problems, several agencies agreed to undertake surveys in response to the invitation of the APU and the Relief and Rehabilitation Commission.

The main objective in 1988 was to undertake rapid assessments of the nutritional situation, including prevalence of wasting, and a review of underlying causes of malnutrition in the community. This information was intended to assist the planning and implementation of the western relief operation.

A second objective was to strengthen the institutional capacity of the Ministry of Health, or other suitable local institution, to co-ordinate and maintain a low-cost system of community-based nutritional surveillance. In 1989, a regular nutrition monitoring programme was set up for the purposes of famine early warning in three of the most food insecure communities in north Darfur.

Lessons learnt

The methods and approach of the new 1988 initiative evolved from the lessons learnt about gathering information in 1984–6 (Box 5.1). The areas to be surveyed were purposively selected from the more food insecure northeast. The limited coverage would allow more in-depth data collection, improved cross checking of findings and faster feedback of results. Longer stays in individual communities would allow survey teams to get to know people in the area and involve them in the surveys and any subsequent activities. Collaboration between agencies was considered vital, with Oxfam, the Sudanese Red Crescent, MSF–Holland, MSF–Belgium and GOAL, all agreeing to participate in nutritional surveillance activities in Darfur. Low operating costs were also a key factor, as they would enable the Ministry of Health to sustain the nutrition survey activities in the future.

Staff and training

Initially, the programme employed just five people: an expatriate nutritionist, two women field-workers who had previously worked as part of the SRC/LRCS nutrition teams in 1986, a driver and a driver's assistant. A Darfuri counterpart to the expatriate nutritionist started work in 1989 and took overall charge of the programme in 1992 after successfully completing a Master's degree in human nutrition.

Box 5.1 Lessons learnt from gathering nutritional information in Darfur, 1984–6

PROBLEM	SOLUTION

Sampling difficulties

One of the most difficult aspects of the surveys was the assembly of an adequate sampling frame (Taylor, 1985). The most recent census data were from 1983, which was generally considered unreliable because of migration within Darfur since then. It was also difficult randomly to sample the children of nomads.

Abandon large-scale cluster surveys in favour of purposive sampling of the worst-affected areas.

Local people were asked the whereabouts of nomads, who were then purposively selected.

Inappropriate scale of coverage

A severe limitation of the region-wide surveys was their level of aggregation. Statistically, anthropometric results could not be disaggregated to examine differences within Darfur. But it was precisely those differences that were of interest for the purposes of targeting and prioritizing delivery of food aid.

Most clusters were selected from the more densely populated western and southern parts of the region. Consequently, the prevalence of malnutrition in Darfur as a whole masked the rapidly developing famine in the north-east. Coverage of surveys was also affected by poor access, with rough terrain hindering travel as well as insecurity making travel unsafe.

Collect data representative of smaller areas allowing a localised view of the nutritional situation (depth rather than breadth). Purposively select communities from the less densely populated north-east (the worst-affected areas).

Limit the number of communities visited, thereby giving more time to negotiate difficult roads to inaccessible areas. Avoid all unnecessary risks associated with insecurity.

Poor timeliness

The large-scale surveys took months rather than weeks to complete. Because of the long lag period between the time data were collected and then reported, the recommendations contained within the reports were already out of date.

Undertake small individual assessments, process results while in the field, provide immediate feedback to the communities and distribute survey reports as quickly as possible (within one to two weeks of returning to El Fasher).

Dubious results—poor reliability

The reliability of the estimates of malnutrition was a controversial issue. There were many inexperienced or unqualified nutritionists undertaking surveys, and their poor application of sampling and measuring techniques cast doubt on their results.

Encourage co-operation and collaboration between participating agencies.

Standardize anthropometric procedures, while allowing flexible methods for collecting other information.

(continued over)

Box 5.1 (cont)

PROBLEM	SOLUTION

Weak interpretation

Few agencies had the technical abilities, much less the experience, to understand and interpret the results of anthropometric surveys in Darfur. Many reports implicitly assumed that growth failure was the outcome of inadequate food intake, to which the automatic response was food aid. Reports rarely considered the impact of infectious disease, or the underlying causes of malnutrition.

Attach equal importance to understanding the underlying causes of malnutrition and to measuring the extent of wasting.

The wealth of quantitative and qualitative information collected was sometimes unwieldy and specific details had to be sacrificed in order to present a general picture.

Pay more attention to learning about seasonal patterns of food security and disease, and their impact on anthropometric status.

The expected seasonal changes in anthropometric status in Darfur were largely unknown. Anthropometric results were obviously high during the famine, but how much higher than 'normal' was anybody's guess.

High costs—low sustainability

None of the surveys in Darfur between 1984 and 1988 would have been possible without the considerable resources committed by international agencies. The highest costs incurred by the NSDMP surveys were for vehicle travel between survey sites, and the cost of outside experts. This level of region-wide surveillance could not have been sustained by the regional government.

Minimize the travel costs of mobile survey teams by limiting the number of sites visited.

Seek help and advice from people in the community and local government rather than being dependent on outsiders.

Establish a more cost-effective community based monitoring programme.

Replace the expatriate nutritionist by a trained and experienced local counterpart.

Survey fatigue

Increasingly mothers refused to co-operate with the nutrition survey teams. Initially there was the incentive that surveys could result in food assistance to the village, but often this did not materialize. There were no obvious benefits of having children weighed and measured, but the drawbacks of inconvenience and distressed children were clear. Resistance of mothers to having their children weighed and measured was far less in Darfur than elsewhere in Sudan. In the Red Sea Hills for example, mothers actively resisted having their children weighed for fear of the 'evil eye' (Shepherd, 1991).

Train field-workers to take account of the views and opinions of local people and to take time to explain what they were doing there. Seek co-operation in a positive way, by encouraging people to participate not only in weighing and measuring, but also in discussing nutritional problems and solutions.

Box 5.2 Summary of methods

RAPID NUTRITION ASSESSMENTS

Selection of villages — Those village councils most affected by food insecurity.

Quantitative methods — Anthropometric measurements of children. Short questionnaires about food security.

Qualitative information — Rapid rural appraisal techniques: secondary data; semi-structured interviewing with focus groups, key informants and selected individuals; observation; wealth ranking.

Analyses, interpretation and report writing — Prevalence rate of wasting and average anthropometric status.
Review of underlying causes (qualitative data).
Discussions with local leaders and regional decision makers.
Standardized reports distributed in El Fasher and Khartoum.

METHODS FOR LONGITUDINAL MONITORING

Selection of sentinel sites — Three towns which had hardly recovered from the 1984–5 famine when they were badly hit by the effects of harvest failure in 1987.

The community monitors — Three volunteers from each town, two women and one man, were trained to weigh and measure children, and also to analyse and interpret the results, taking particular account of seasonal effects.

Quantitative methods — Anthropometric measurements of the children from 50 households selected at random every three to four months for one year. A new sample was selected for the following year. Interviews with mothers.

Qualitative information — Semi-structured interviews, based on a check-list which covered the underlying causes of malnutrition.

Report writing — Results on a summary sheet, which was sent to El Fasher, together with the raw data. Standardized reports on each round of monitoring were disseminated to agencies, ministries and donors in Darfur and Khartoum.

Volunteers enlisted from the community helped out during the surveys. Sometimes experienced staff from other agencies joined the Oxfam team, especially if they had a good knowledge of the people or area to be visited.

The nutritionist in charge of the programme trained the field-workers, who in turn trained the local volunteers. The training included both anthropometric assessments (measurement techniques, manual and computer analysis, report writing) and also how to examine the underlying causes of malnutrition at the level of the community.

Methods

The methods for the rapid nutrition assessments and the longitudinal monitoring are described in detail in Appendix 1, and summarized in Box 5.2. Both approaches used a combination of quantitative and qualitative methods.

Trends in nutrition and food security, 1987–90

By 1987 food security in Darfur was already weakened by the impact of drought in the mid-seventies and had barely recovered from the devastation caused by the 1984–5 famine. For many tribes this led to a transformation in their traditional way of life as they sought alternative sources of income and food. In the years that followed 1987, three out of four harvests in Darfur either partially or completely failed. Most of what is known about food security and nutrition at that time was learnt through the work of the Agricultural Planning Unit and the nutritional surveillance programme.

This case-study looks at local food security in three towns, Malha, Mareiga and Cuma, in the north-east of Darfur. The standard early warning indicators monitored by the APU present a region-wide picture of food security, while the nutritional assessments and monitoring provide a localized view, and show the impact of weakened food security on people's lives and the anthropometric status of their children.

Apart from anthropometric data, the nutrition monitoring programme collected information about the response of local people to deteriorating food security. This included labour migration, collection of wild foods and low-status trading. The assessments also examined the health environment, and quality of the diet (access to milk). This combination of local community-level information with region-wide indicators was one of the strengths of the information system in Darfur.

In Darfur as a whole, agricultural production is the backbone of food security, and if that fails then all other aspects of food security are affected. The poor harvest of 1987 was followed by a very good harvest in 1988, a partly failed harvest in 1989 and almost complete failure in 1990. The failed harvests were the result of low rainfall which was poorly distributed

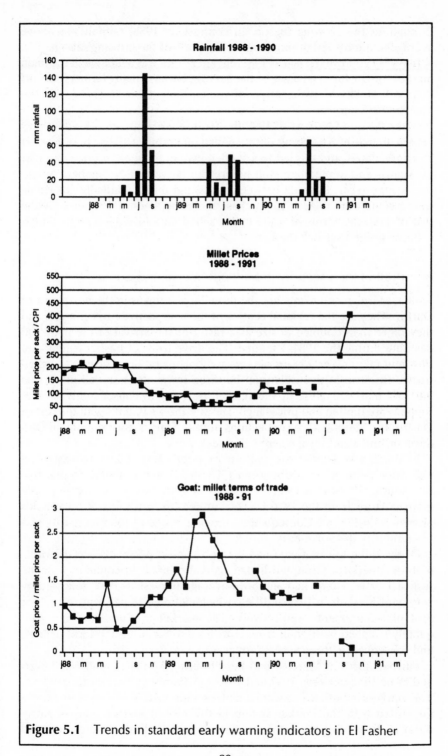

Figure 5.1 Trends in standard early warning indicators in El Fasher

throughout the growing season. In contrast, in 1988, rainfall was above average and most fell during August, the peak of the growing season.

In a very good year, such as 1988, cheaper grain was available in the main markets of Darfur in advance of the harvest, because many farmers sold off their old stocks in anticipation of replenishing their reserves with the bumper 1988 harvest.

After the good harvest of 1988 the food security situation became progressively worse. As a result of the inadequate rains of 1989 a poor harvest was anticipated, and this led to a sudden leap in the market price of millet in August and September, well before the harvest in November. As expected, the terms of trade between goats and millet gradually got worse (more goats were needed to purchase the same amount of grain). By the end of 1990 the terms of trade had reached an all-time low, signalling a collapse in the livestock market.

A portrait of food security in Malha, Mareiga and Cuma

Malha, Mareiga and Cuma are the three largest towns in the north-east of Darfur. They are the regional centres of their respective rural councils and they more than doubled in size as a result of the arrival of the poor and destitute during the 1984–5 famine. The drive from El Fasher is long and slow and takes several hours across sandy plains or along deeply trenched tracks. Because of this isolation, the three towns are not well integrated into the market system of the rest of Darfur and consequently market supplies are limited and prices high. Despite the weak links with the rest of Darfur, the Meidob have connections outside Darfur, for example, in Omdurman, and also Libya, where many seek work.

In north-east Darfur the pattern of poor rains, failed harvests and escalating price of cereals between 1988 and 1990 was similar to that further south, but more extreme. Households in the north-east did not have grain in store from the 1986 harvest, unlike up to a third of households elsewhere in Darfur. Consequently, the magnitude of food insecurity was far greater in the north-east.

Of the three towns, Cuma had the best harvest prospects because of its more southerly position and higher annual rainfall. In common with the rest of Darfur, Cuma had an above-average harvest in 1988, followed by very poor harvests in 1989 and 1990 which met only 14 per cent and 12 per cent of requirements, respectively. The market in Cuma was not adequately supplied with grain from elsewhere to make up the local deficits, and consequently there were shortages.

Further north in Mareiga and neighbouring Malha rainfall was lower, and at no time between 1987 and 1990 was there any harvest to speak of. The markets in both towns were unable to supply grain as they were poorly integrated with the market system in the rest of Darfur. This is partly because distances between these markets and El Fasher were long, and transport costs high. Also, demand was unpredictable as purchasing power was low (Buchanan-Smith, 1989). A small supply of grain was available from traders travelling between Omdurman and Mellit, where they purchased goods from Libya. This supply was small, irregular and limited to the dry season when travel was easier.

Because of the shortages, a sack of millet cost up to four times more in these northern communities than in El Fasher. Although millet was always more expensive in Malha and Mareiga, the terms of trade were not always inferior because goats fetched a higher price than in El Fasher (at least to begin with). By August 1989, terms of trade in the north-east deteriorated to the same level as in El Fasher.

Local strategies in response to food insecurity

People were compelled by food insecurity to find additional ways of securing an adequate living. This included migration in search of work, collection of wild foods and petty trading. Many of these activities were regularly undertaken by a small proportion of the population, but as the pressure of food insecurity increased so the numbers involved in these low-status activities grew.

Labour migration

Previously, very few Meidob left their homeland in search of work, but labour migration became increasingly common following the heavy livestock losses during the famine. Between 1988 and 1990 approximately 16 per cent of households in Malha, and 7 per cent of households in Mareiga and Cuma had male family members in Libya, where they might stay for several years. This contributed to a growing number of women-headed households.

Seasonal migration in search of agricultural work was less important; in 1988 between 4 per cent and 11 per cent of households reported family members to be working elsewhere in Darfur. This included small groups of women travelling together. In subsequent years the poor harvest throughout Darfur meant this type of work was unavailable.

In all three towns, paid work shepherding livestock often took men or even entire households away from home for months at a time or even longer. Strictly speaking, this is not a type of labour migration as the work was found at home.

Elsewhere in Darfur, tribes follow different patterns of labour migration. For example, among the Berti, migration to Libya was rare, while long-term migration to Khartoum or the Gulf States had been taking place for several decades. In Umm Keddada area council, cash crops, in particular groundnuts, were grown in the south but not in the north, and as a result southwards migration in search of seasonal agricultural work was common.

Small trades

In Malha, in 1988, only 2 per cent of households were involved in cutting wood or grass for resale, while in Cuma 61 per cent of households traded wood and grass.

In Cuma, handicrafts were an important source of income for almost half the women interviewed (42 per cent). The carpets, leatherwork and mats produced in Cuma were well known. This small cottage industry received some support from NGOs.

An additional source of trade in Cuma was catering for the needs of travellers as Cuma was an important stopping point on the route between El Fasher and Khartoum during the rainy season. There were several tea shops and restaurants, and many individual food vendors.

Wild foods

The most common distress food eaten in the famine of 1984–5 throughout northern Darfur was 'mukheit' (*Boscia senegaliensis*).[3] During the 1984–5 famine, *mukheit* was eaten by 94 per cent of households in North Darfur who had access to it (de Waal, 1989a). After the famine, people in the west of Darfur stopped collecting *mukheit*. In contrast, in the more food insecure north-east, *mukheit* was collected regularly every year between March and November, and either eaten during the hungry season or stored as a food reserve. Thus an unpalatable distress food had become a regular part of the diet.

The consumption of *mukheit* in Malha and Mareiga reflected the degree of food insecurity. As food security deteriorated after 1988, the proportion of households consuming *mukheit* rose dramatically (Figure 5.2) to more than 80 per cent of all households interviewed.

Usually *mukheit* berries are collected for personal use, but during the 1984–5 famine, *mukheit* was sold in local markets and often replaced grain as the staple food. Trading of *mukheit* was not seen again until the end of 1990, when once again no grain was available and so *mukheit* was the only available staple food. However, the rains in 1990 were so poor that even the harvest of *mukheit* was very small.

Another sign of worsening food insecurity in Mareiga in 1990 was the proportion of *mukheit* in the diet. For many households, cereal reserves had run out and *mukheit* had become the only available staple food. As *mukheit* was no longer supplementing a cereal grain, the boiled berries were eaten whole.

---

[3] To collect and process *mukheit* requires a lot of effort. The *mukheit* is picked and sun dried to make removal of the seed coat easier. Shelled *mukheit* can be stored for several years. Careful preparation, which involves soaking in regular changes of water for several days, is needed to remove toxins. The soaked berries are boiled for up to three hours until soft, and then dried and ground into flour which is used to supplement millet flour. Neither the cooked berries nor the millet/*mukheit* porridge are particularly palatable.

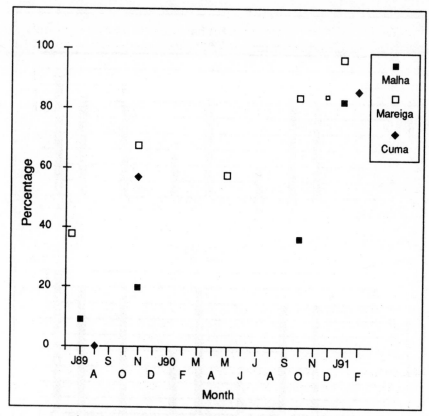

Figure 5.2 Percentage of households eating *mukheit*

Other wild foods
Other wild foods used by people in Malha and Mareiga in 1988 and 1989 included 'dirassa' and 'koreb'. These were available in much smaller quantities than *mukheit* as they were more dependent on the rains. Hence fewer people were found to be using them. *Dirassa* is a thorny grass seed and the removal of the seed from the thorns requires great patience and care.

In 1989, *koreb* collected from neighbouring Dar Zaghawa was available for sale in Malha market. In Mareiga in the same year *koreb* was reportedly growing in nearby wadis up to four days travel away.

Watermelon was often intercropped with millet and although it is not a wild food as such, the seeds were used as a distress food to make up shortages of grain, and were frequently stored in anticipation of a period of acute food insecurity. Seeds were either stored as dried whole pieces of watermelon (Kutum rural council in 1990), or were separated and dried (Umm Keddada, Malha and Mareiga, 1988 to 1990). The dried watermelon flesh could be added to millet porridge to sweeten it, and the seeds were pounded to remove the seed coat, and ground up for making 'medida' (soup).

93

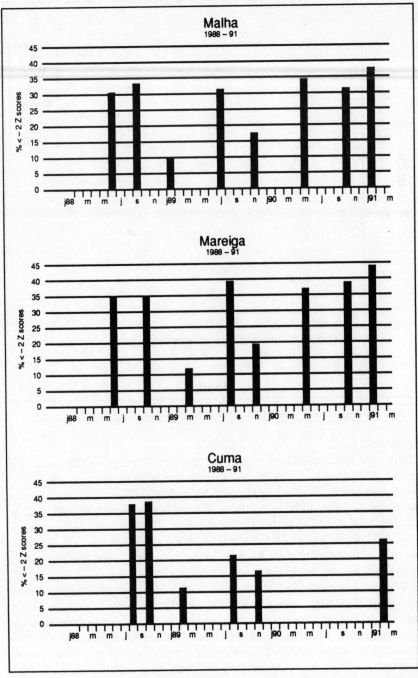

Figure 5.3 Prevalence of malnutrition in Malha, Mareiga and Cuma
(percentage below –2 Z scores weight-for-height)

94

Sensitivity of nutritional status to seasonal changes in food security: 1988 to 1990

The children of Malha, Mareiga and Cuma gained or lost weight in relation to the seasonal patterns of food security. In general the patterns of nutritional status in all three towns were similar but not always identical because of slight local differences.

Anthropometric status was usually at its best in the months following the harvest, and then gradually declined reaching its lowest point during the rainy season before the next harvest (the hungry season) (Figure 5.3).

1987–8

Eight months after the failed 1987 harvest, the prevalence of malnutrition in Malha and Mareiga was alarmingly high: 30.6 per cent in Malha and 34.2 per cent in Mareiga. These high rates are indicative of a particularly severe hungry season caused by the poor harvest of the previous year.

1988–9

Most of Darfur had a good harvest in November 1988 and as a result, by the beginning of 1989, the rate of malnutrition dropped sharply by more than 20 per cent. In Cuma, for example, the rate dropped from 38.1 per cent to 11.3 per cent, and the mean nutritional status improved from –1.7 to –1.1 Z scores. This remarkable recovery was attributed to the bumper harvest and better market conditions.

In Cuma, grain production was sufficient to meet annual requirements. While this was not true for Malha and Mareiga, grain prices fell. Good pasture conditions were maintained well into the dry season and livestock were kept near the villages until early 1989, which increased the availability of milk.

Following the 1988 harvest, the generally improved food security throughout Darfur reduced the severity of the following hungry season. In Cuma, for example, 37.7 per cent were malnourished in August 1988, while significantly fewer (20.7 per cent) were malnourished in August 1989. But pockets of severe food insecurity were still to be found; in Malha and Mareiga the hungry season of 1989 was as severe as the previous year and rates of malnutrition were again above 30 per cent. The main problem facing these towns was the supply of grain. Supply problems were exacerbated by the effects of the *coup d'état* in June. Traders ceased operating as they waited for the new government's price policy to be made known. In July 1989, no grain had been available in Mareiga for more than a month and before that only sporadic supplies came from Omdurman or by camel from nearby areas. Grain supply in Malha was slightly better, although millet prices were still higher than in Cuma and further south.

1989–90

Even though the harvest of 1989 was poor, it was followed by a seasonal decrease in the prevalence of malnutrition, even in Malha and Mareiga.

But the expected simultaneous decrease in millet prices did not occur. The fall in the rate of malnutrition may have been partly due to more milk and meat being available for a short period during the rainy season. Some of the animals belonged to members of the Meidob tribe from villages north of Malha and Mareiga who had started to migrate southwards by November because of poor pasture conditions.[4] In Cuma, cows were kept near the settlement most of the year, and there would have been a good supply of milk during the rainy season.

Despite the initial improvements in nutritional status following the 1989 harvest, it was not long before it started to decline once more. By the time of the next rainy season, anthropometric status was well below normal for the time of year. People from Malha and Mareiga had difficulty purchasing grain from Mellit as the local government had imposed trading restrictions across rural council boundaries. Sales of grain to people from outside Mellit rural council were limited to two sacks per household, whereas previously people from Malha and Mareiga would travel to Mellit and purchase grain on behalf of several families. Transport of grain to Malha and Mareiga markets was also reduced because of fuel shortages. In Malha terms of trade deteriorated further.

1990–91

In anticipation of an even worse harvest than the previous year there was a huge leap in millet prices around October 1990, and the livestock markets collapsed. No grain at all was available in the markets in Mellit area council. On average the price of one sack of millet in North Darfur rose to more than LS 1 000 by October. At the same time prices of sheep and goats decreased by more than 75 per cent. 1991 was expected to be a famine year by many in the region.

In contrast to the expected seasonal pattern, the high rate of wasting found during the hungry season in 1990 was maintained after the harvest. The severity of food insecurity eliminated the expected seasonal decrease in wasting. Children did not make their usual rapid recovery from the effects of the hungry season and were approaching the coming hungry season in an extremely vulnerable state.

This overview of rates of malnutrition and food security shows how the nutritional status of children in these communities was sensitive to changes in food security. This can also be illustrated by the distribution curve of the anthropometric status of all children. The entire curve shifted to the left or right in response to changes in the local food security situation[5] (Figure 5.4).

---

[4] After good rains, southward migration does not start until February/March the following year.
[5] The prevalence of wasting (below –2 scores WFH) focuses on changes to the left-hand side of the distribution curve, which overlooks the weight changes experienced by most children.

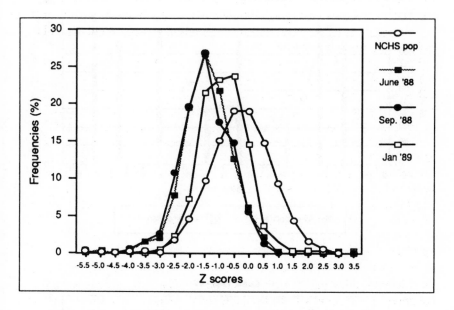

Figure 5.4   Frequency distribution of Z scores in three surveys
in Malha

We are fairly certain that changes in the nutritional status of children in
the Darfur villages were not caused by changes in disease patterns, but
were the result of seasonal and unseasonal patterns of food security. The
seasonal changes in the weight of children were dramatic; the longitudinal
monitoring showed that virtually every child lost weight or failed to gain
weight during the rainy season and underwent a rapid recovery following
the harvest. These changes mirrored the severity of food insecurity. In
those villages where food insecurity was more pronounced, the rate of
malnutrition was indeed higher.

With the possible exception of measles, it is unlikely that disease could
bring about such dramatic changes in the prevalence of malnutrition, often
by more than 20 per cent. The effect of diarrhoea on weight gain tends to be
transient, and cannot be detected after a few weeks (Briend *et al.*, 1989a).

The early rapid nutritional assessments found that about 25 per cent of
children suffered symptoms of disease which would not account for a
change in weight in all children. We concluded that disease was likely to
be important in determining who became malnourished but was not responsible for the overall decline in anthropometric status.

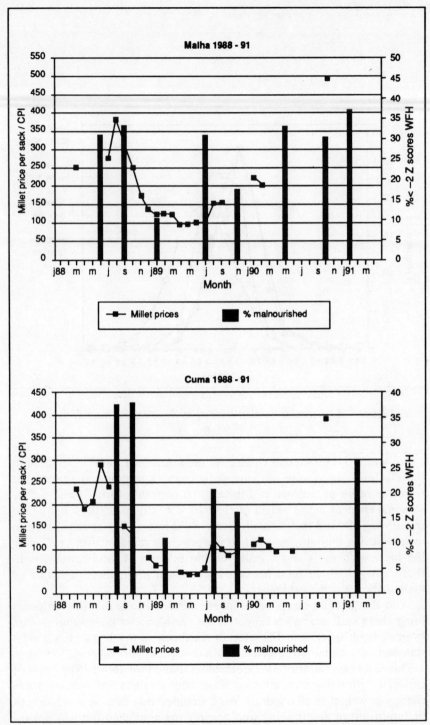

Figure 5.5 Malnutrition and millet prices in Malha and Cuma

Timeliness of nutritional data as an indicator of food security: 1988 to 1990

The prevalence of malnutrition moved in the same direction as millet prices, while the mean anthropometric status moved in the same direction as market prices and terms of trade. As grain prices dropped in early 1989, the prevalence of wasting decreased and rose again from the middle of 1989 as market prices increased. The exception to this pattern was in November 1989 in Malha, where following the poor harvest there was the expected seasonal decrease in wasting, but millet prices continued to rise as a consequence of the poor harvest. By May the following year, the prevalence of wasting had increased to more than 30 per cent.

Both market prices and anthropometric status changed at about the same time and there did not appear to be a lag between an increase in market prices and a fall in nutritional status. This strongly suggests that the weight-for-height indicator can give a timely indication of changes in food security in these communities.

Why did nutrition fail to improve?

Despite the various achievements over the three years of the case study, food security and nutrition failed to improve. The communities were powerless to affect the deeper basic causes of malnutrition, which could only be addressed at a national level. At the beginning of the case-study in early 1988, Darfur was in overall food deficit and the government and donors were committed to making up the food shortfall and targeting relief where necessary. But the subsequent 'Western relief operation' failed both in getting food from central Sudan to Darfur, and in targeting it at those most in need.[6]

The food deficit worsened following harvest failure in 1989 and 1990, but this time the Darfur early warning system failed to elicit a response from national government or donors. The food deficit was not compensated for by movements of food into the region, either privately or through state interventions. In north-east Darfur food security deteriorated and the case-study villages received little support from outside.

Causes of malnutrition

The key underlying cause of malnutrition in North Darfur was food insecurity. The case-study communities were food insecure because of a lack of

---

[6] The principle of targeting in the Western relief operation was agreed but there were no clear guide-lines on how to target in practice. Political pressure influenced geographical targeting, so that at the village level distributions tended to be shared out among the whole population, rather than distributed according to need. As a result, grain was distributed very thinly and the impact on individual households was probably negligible.

assets, geographic isolation, poor transport links, lack of alternative sources of income and the debilitating effects of previous droughts. These combined factors made them vulnerable to seasonal food shortages, which were grossly exaggerated by drought. The other two underlying causes of malnutrition (care of women and children, and the health environment and access to health services) had a relatively small impact on nutritional status.

Child care was obviously affected by food security, as people were consciously reducing their food intake, not through ignorance or lack of education, but as a strategy for surviving a period of severe hardship while protecting their future livelihood. Access to milk was affected by the strategy of sending livestock away from the home in search of water and pasture. Provision of health services in all three villages was weak, and the supply of essential drugs was very poor, although free of charge when available. This meant that both rich and poor households shared the same limited facilities.

The underlying causes of malnutrition were exacerbated by the basic causes of malnutrition operating at the regional and national level. There was an obvious lack of resources including economic resources, organizational resources (public service infrastructure), and human resources. The macro-economy was weak, and political factors had a major influence on events.

The local communities were unable to bring about significant changes to public service infrastructure, markets and employment. They could only address the immediate effects of drought within their villages. Community leaders planned and organized local initiatives to reduce the impact of food insecurity on the poorer households and more vulnerable groups. They collected funds locally and started supplementary feeding programmes, but faced with an enormous need and without any external support, these local funds did not last long. Unless the basic causes of malnutrition are addressed at a national level, interventions at community level are going to be severely hampered by obstacles beyond people's influence and control.

Discoveries about malnutrition, wealth and food security

Wealth ranking of individual households revealed important details about differences in wealth and food security between households in the same village. Wealth ranking was undertaken by local informants, who used their own definition of wealth and their personal knowledge of the local community to classify households into wealth groups (Grandin, 1988). Wealth ranking takes into account the multiple determinants of poverty which are unique to a given situation.

Wealth ranking was first used to evaluate a targeted food distribution programme in Malha, Mareiga and Cuma in 1988. It was used again in 1989 to examine the wealth characteristics of the random sample of families whose children were included in the longitudinal monitoring programme.

The results of this simple procedure were a revelation; they showed how wealth was perceived by local people, and revealed that differences in wealth within the communities had no significant impact on nutritional status. Malnourished children were found in all wealth groups, and no relationship was found between children's nutritional status and family wealth in the most food insecure part of North Darfur over a period of two years.

The local informants used more than one indicator to distinguish between the wealth status of the families. Wealth was mainly defined by a family having more than one source of income, which always included large numbers of livestock. For example, in Cuma most rich families owned about 30 to 40 sheep, and some owned more than 100. In Mareiga most rich households owned between 10 and 15 camels and more than 10 goats. These richer households did not cultivate millet, and other sources of income were obtained from business as merchants, shopkeepers or road haulage. Not all merchants were in the richer wealth group.

Local informants defined poverty using a wide range of indicators: loss of livestock, small farms, large number of dependants including wives and children, the elderly without adult children to support them, dependence on others, reliance on petty trading of grass and wood, casual labouring and charcoal cutting. Poverty was relative, even within such a small area as Mellit area council. Families classified as poor in Cuma would almost certainly have been ranked in the medium wealth group in Malha and Mareiga.

There are several likely explanations for the presence of malnourished children in rich and poor households in the Darfur villages. The most important explanation is that the reduction of food intake was an almost universal response to the worsening food security situation. The poorest people had few options available to them and probably had few other choices but to go hungry. For the rich, eating less may have been an early and voluntary response to food insecurity, as they chose not to make use of their other available options.

This partly reflects the priority given to preserving capital and other assets needed to ensure their future livelihood. One factor that discouraged sales of livestock unless absolutely necessary was the unfavourable terms of trade for converting livestock to grain. Also, the wealth bound up in livestock is not as accessible as stores of grain or cash. It is not as easy to convert livestock into an immediate source of food or income, particularly during drought when animals are taken to distant parts in search of pasture and water, by either a hired shepherd or member of the houshold. So the members of the household, women and children in particular, would be separated from the household's assets, unable to convert them to cash or to use them as a supply of milk or meat. In some cases poorer families had equal, if not better, access to milk than richer families. In Cuma, for example, poor families owned only a small number of goats but because they kept them close to their homes, they had access to fresh milk.

The social and kinship networks operating within the community may also partly explain why malnourished children were found in all wealth strata. There were often social forces at work which obliged richer households to support poorer households.[7] Claims on other households, patrons, or even on government and the international community are a type of entitlement (Swift, 1989). In a few cases in the Darfur villages, rich households were obliged to support poor households because they were fostering their children. Poorer households made claims on the available assets of richer families, or obtained credit from richer relatives, which due to circumstances had to be written-off as bad debts.

The important point learnt from wealth ranking is that the localized impact of food insecurity on the nutritional status of children far outweighed any effect resulting from differences in wealth in the community. Seasonal and unseasonal changes in food security in these villages affected everybody. Findings on malnutrition, wealth and food security are presented in more detail by Jaspars and Young (in preparation).

---

[7] Watts (1988) describes these obligations as a 'social field of force' or 'moral economy'.

PART 3

NUTRITION AND FAMINE

The way forward

CHAPTER 6

A new way of looking at nutrition in famine

Introduction

Nutrition is a key factor in assessment and response to famine, whatever the cause. But the current view of the role of nutrition is so limited and narrow that it cannot hope to have any more than a very limited and temporary impact on nutritional problems. Entitlement theory and the work on coping strategies has enormously advanced our understanding of the cause of famine (Chapter 1). Demographers and epidemiologists have revealed much about the causes and patterns of famine mortality. Recent work on the political economy of famine has highlighted the political dimensions of complex emergencies. But this new knowledge has yet to have much of an impact on either nutritional assessments of famine or actual intervention programmes. In practice, misplaced assumptions about hunger, starvation and death continue to dictate and limit the scope of nutritional assessments and interventions.

This chapter aims to address this problem by developing the model of nutrition and famine presented in Chapter 1 which provides a new way of looking at the role of nutrition in times of food insecurity and famine. The practical implications of the model and our analysis of nutrition in famine are discussed in the second part of the chapter. This includes interpretation of the results of nutritional assessments, assessment methods, seeking more appropriate interventions at an earlier stage of famine and targeting interventions.

The purpose of the model

The purpose of a model or conceptual framework like the one in Figure 6.1 is to show the relationship between different factors and how they affect one another and thereby bring about change. If the process of change is to be modified in any way, the first vital step is a better understanding of how and why it comes about.

There are many factors involved in the complex process leading to famine, and the final outcomes of famines are rarely exactly the same. In the worst circumstances there may be many thousands of famine-related deaths, but in other famines mortality rates may even improve temporarily. Famine disrupts people's way of life as their entitlements are radically affected: crops fail, food shortages force up market prices, the labour market contracts and so on. Distress migration of whole households brings

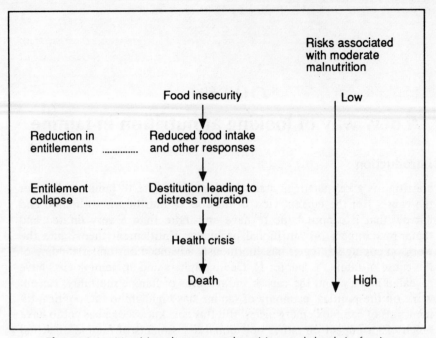

Figure 6.1 Nutritional status, malnutrition and death in famine: a conceptual framework (repeat of Figure 1.4)

with it the chaos and confusion of social disruption and multiplying health risks as people are less able to care for themselves in an increasingly hostile environment. Unravelling the potential health risks and the economic risks to people's livelihoods, both immediately and in the future, is a difficult task. Additional difficulties of inadequate or inappropriate information, which has apparently little bearing on the immediate situation, compounds the problems.

The purpose of the model developed in Chapter 1 is to shed light on the relationship between nutritional status, malnutrition, food security and the risk of famine deaths. A better understanding leads to more informed choices and decisions and so subsequent actions are more likely to achieve their objectives. So whose objectives and actions are we talking about? We believe this model will prove useful to anyone who has the least concern with eradicating the suffering and deprivation of famine. This includes those organizations, institutions and individuals working to relieve the effects of food insecurity and famine, or working to prevent its recurrence. It also includes those people directly affected by famine. They are on the receiving end of well-meaning famine relief projects and interventions. If these programmes are based on a poor understanding of the local dynamics of famine, the resulting programmes will be of little benefit to local people, and they are more likely to cause additional problems. The very least that can be expected from a better understanding of famine is the improved use of resources for emergency relief.

106

The following sections provide a review of the conceptual framework of nutrition in famine and go on to explain the implications of the framework for methods of nutritional assessment, interpretation of results and the implications for famine relief interventions.

The early and late stages of famine

The model distinguishes between the early and late stages of famine. In general people are home based during the early stages of famine, while in the final stages large numbers of people have migrated to relief camps.

In the early stages, drought and crop failure erodes people's entitlements and threatens their food security. In response, they must adopt various coping strategies. With passing time, their endurance is stretched and sooner or later people are forced to adopt strategies that are increasingly harmful to their way of life. For example, the sale of productive assets erodes people's future livelihoods and brings destitution that much closer. There are also the costs to the environment, as more and more people are forced to over-exploit the local natural resources. Over-cultivation of marginal land—not leaving a long enough fallow period—and excessive tree cutting, degrade the soil and rapidly lead to desertification. This environmental damage cannot easily be restored and so affects the lives of future generations. The early stages of famine can go on for many years without developing into the catastrophic final stages of famine when many people die.

If conditions do not improve, destitution becomes unavoidable for more and more households as their remaining entitlements are no longer able to sustain even the most basic level of food security. A collapse in entitlements leaves people no other choice but to starve or to migrate. Many of the destitute leave their homes in desperation and end up in famine camps. The social disruption of distress migration and the creation of famine camps represent the final stage of famine.

Public health problems are very often concentrated in a relief camp, especially in those camps that are newly formed, although some assistance is likely to be available. Inevitably, spontaneous settlements are disorganized and chaotic; adequate shelter, food, water and sanitation are all lacking. Even though people may have been reasonably healthy when they arrived, the poor health environment means it is not long before they are affected. This is particularly true of the nutritional status of children, which very often declines soon after arrival in a relief camp.

After the crisis is over, conditions rarely revert to how they were before. Many households and communities are usually greatly impoverished as a result of famine, and are increasingly vulnerable. Their livelihoods may be wrecked and may take years to recover, if they ever do. At this stage 'rehabilitation' programmes are aimed at helping people to get back on their feet and reduce their vulnerability to future episodes of famine.

107

If these rehabilitation programmes fail and people are unable to recover a viable livelihood they could potentially be entering the early stages of a new famine. This in fact is what happens in parts of Africa. The famine process becomes a cycle that repeats itself every so many years, rather than a linear process as we have represented it. With every new cycle, the process becomes shorter as people are less able to cope. To break this cycle and prevent famine, a new approach and more appropriate interventions are needed in the early stages of famine, or during the recovery phase after the health crisis.

Local variations

The model is not definitive. It is not intended to tell you exactly how famine will progress, but provides a framework for understanding famine and the aims of relief interventions.

The threat of destitution is likely to vary for different groups of people depending on their individual circumstances, particularly their livelihoods and the resources available to them. At any one point in time, there are those who are already destitute and are experiencing the later stages of famine, and those who are still able to support themselves by means of various coping strategies. Those who have been impoverished from past episodes of famine, may have fewer strategies left to cope with food insecurity and so their timing and flexibility in using these strategies changes. For example, the sequence of events in the framework may be repeated, but the stages will occur in quicker succession as people move faster down the sequence, or even start midway in the sequence.

The sequence of events described in the framework may vary, for example, in some cases distress migration may occur as a result of lack of water rather than a reduced entitlement to food. Reduction in food intake early on in the famine process may not be a general phenomenon, and differences between locations, groups of people, and also within households should be expected. Not all households may choose to reduce their food intake early on, while some households may choose to feed preferentially certain family members, for example, children or wage earners.

Complex emergencies in war situations may start by following this pattern, as conflict forces people to relocate themselves either within their own country or beyond its borders. But following the acute phase of displacement, people are often unable to return to their homes and have to rely almost entirely on outside support for their basic needs. These protracted emergencies, which can last several years, are increasing in number, and in terms of funding commitments surpass short-term emergencies. In 1990, commitments of the World Food Programme for protracted operations came to a total of $335.6 million world-wide, whereas commitments for emergency operations came to $132 million (WFP, 1991).

108

The early stages of famine—nutritional status as an indicator of food security

People affected by famine are not passive victims of forces beyond their control; people have choices, some more than others. As the effects of drought begin to be felt, people respond according to their priorities and the options open to them. One of the first responses is often dietary change: eating less or switching to inferior food. In the short-term, people experience hunger, but in the long-term they will have managed to preserve valuable resources and so prevent loss of livelihood and destitution. The short-term cost of hunger is therefore preferable to the long-term costs of asset depletion and loss of livelihood. This cutting back on food in the early stages of famine is very different from the starvation forced on the destitute, who have no choices.

In north-east Darfur the nutritional status of children responded very quickly to changes in food security. As the situation worsened, the prevalence of wasting increased, mean nutritional status dropped and the entire distribution curve of nutritional status shifted over to the left (Figure 5.4, Chapter 5). As the situation improved, the opposite happened within a matter of weeks. Nutritional data from the first two years of the case-study crudely illustrates the normal seasonal pattern: an increase in the prevalence of malnutrition during the hungry season prior to the harvest, and a significant decline thereafter. Food security deteriorated during the latter two years of the case-study. Harvest failure in 1990 meant that the normal post-harvest reduction in malnutrition was negligible, and was insignificant compared with the post-harvest reduction in malnutrition levels in 1988. These changes were a result of changing food security rather than changes in incidence of disease (see Chapter 5, page 95–9).

Both seasonal and unseasonal patterns of food security were reflected by the prevalence of acute malnutrition. The changes in nutritional status occurred at about the same time as changes in other important early warning indicators, in particular market prices of cereals (Chapter 5, page 99). So in Darfur, a high prevalence of malnutrition was not a late indicator of famine, as it occurred far in advance of a 'famine that kills'.

Other examples of dramatic changes in nutritional status in response to a changing food security situation were given in Chapter 2. The view that malnutrition is one of the final outcomes of famine and is accompanied by famine deaths, is very misleading.[1] High rates of malnutrition do not

---

[1] This view largely originates from Sen's entitlement theory, which is the most widely accepted concept of famine. This theory suggests that the sequence of events leading to famine deaths is: impoverishment, destitution, starvation and death. People are not expected to reduce their food intake until they absolutely have no other choice, in other words, after destitution, which would be closely followed by death. The possibility that people may choose not to use their entitlements to food is purposely ignored by Sen in his analysis, although he comments that early reduction in consumption might be the result of ignorance, bad food habits or apathy.

necessarily characterize a famine, nor is famine necessarily accompanied by high malnutrition levels. However, the nutritional status of children under five years can be used as a sensitive and timely indicator of food security.

Famine deaths—nutritional status as an indicator of mortality risk?

People do not usually die as a result of famine until the late stages when severe social disruption leads to a serious deterioration in the local health environment, which increases exposure to infectious disease. In those famines in which a long period of drought is broken by particularly heavy rains, an unusually severe outbreak of malaria may mean that the highest excess mortality occurs after food security conditions have improved (see Chapter 1 page 20).

The risks of disease and death associated with acute malnutrition (wasting) depend largely on the prevailing patterns of disease, which are determined by the health environment. Other nutritional factors also influence excess mortality, in particular breast-feeding and weaning practices, and the nutritional quality of the diet.

In the early stages of famine, drought may temporarily reduce exposure to disease because of the hot dry conditions, in which case a high prevalence of wasting will not be associated with excess deaths. In contrast, in the poor health environment of a famine camp, intense exposure to disease is compounded by high rates of malnutrition and other nutritional factors. Increased vulnerability associated with malnutrition acts in synergy with the increased exposure to disease in a poor health environment to bring about even more deaths than if either factor were found in isolation.

So nutritional status is not a good indicator of mortality risk because the risk associated with any given level of nutritional status is liable to change depending on the local circumstances. Examples of the changing relationship between nutritional status and mortality risk are given in Chapter 1, page 22.

The main reasons for this changing relationship are:

o the health environment (which determines the patterns and incidence of disease)
o access to appropriate health services
o other nutritional factors including breast-feeding and availability of essential micro-nutrients.

There are many nutritional factors that affect mortality risk that are not necessarily associated with growth failure. Improvements to vitamin-A status, for example, reduces mortality risk significantly without affecting growth status. Relief food aid rations are very often deficient in essential micro-nutrients, and there is considerable evidence that the poor

110

nutritional quality of the food rations has caused the outbreak of many deficiency diseases (discussed later).

The practical application of the model

The conceptual framework, 'Nutritional status, malnutrition and death in famine' has major implications for famine assessment and response. These are discussed below, together with practical suggestions as to how the new approach might be applied to assessments and surveillance.

Implications of the new approach for planning assessments

Too often, the objectives of nutritional assessments have not been thought through properly because famine is poorly understood in terms of its causes, development and outcomes. If famine is seen as destitution leading to starvation and death, with malnutrition being one of the final outcomes, then increasing rates of malnutrition will be interpreted as evidence of a growing risk of famine deaths. Obviously, from what we have learnt earlier about famine and nutrition, this is not only simplistic but also quite false.

The conceptual framework in Figure 6.1 shows how famine can be a long drawn-out process which does not always culminate in excess deaths. Early on, people have a number of options and make trade-offs between hunger in the short-term and damage to livelihoods in the long-term. The model shows how the mortality risk associated with a high rate of wasting is likely to increase as the poor health environment intensifies exposure to disease. In relation to this framework, realistic objectives of nutritional assessments are presented in Box 6.1.

Information from a wide range of sources is needed to meet these objectives, especially the last two. To help sort out what is needed to assess, we have used the broad categories of the UNICEF framework (Figure 1.2,

---

Box 6.1 Realistic objectives of nutritional assessments

o Assess changes in nutritional status in relation to normal seasonal patterns.
o Assess whether eating less or dietary change is an early response to food insecurity.
o Assess the underlying causes of malnutrition: food security, health and the health environment and maternal and child care.
o Assess the impact of war, drought or other key events on the food security of particular social or ethnic groups in the population.
o Assess the likelihood of food insecurity worsening.
o Determine the approximate stage of the famine process, and therefore the most appropriate interventions.
o Assess the health risks associated with a given rate of malnutrition in a particular location.

Box 6.2   What to assess

Nutritional status
How does nutritional status usually fluctuate at different times of the year? What other nutritional problems occur on a seasonal basis?

Disease
What diseases are prevalent at different times of the year? Check whether there has been an outbreak of measles which would have affected nutritional status dramatically. If not, disease would not be expected to bring about large changes in nutritional status, say more than 10 to 20 percentage points. In the absence of an outbreak of measles or other major epidemic, a significant change in wasting is likely to be due to food security, especially if the nutritional status of the entire population changes (the frequency distribution curve shifts either to the left or to the right).

Household food security
What are the basic production systems? What are the coping strategies and different sources of food available to each production system? How does the seasonal cycle of activities affect household food security and composition of the diet? How have these been affected or how could they be affected by drought, war, etc.?

The health environment and access to health services
What are the key environmental factors contributing to disease? (Rainfall; water supply; sanitation; inadequate housing; hot, dry and dusty conditions; crowding.) How adequate are the local health services, in terms of immunization coverage, availability of essential drugs, personnel trained in the rational use of drugs, realistic cost of services, access to facilities? How have these been affected by war, civil unrest or other key developments?

Maternal and child care[2]
What are the normal patterns of breast-feeding and weaning? Who shares the responsibility for child care? What constraints do women face in providing adequate care for their children? How has war or drought affected local security and social stability? How has this affected the vulnerability of different groups?

The views of local people and their response to the current episode of food insecurity
What are their immediate concerns and priorities? How do they see the current situation in relation to past episodes of food insecurity? Consider the views of different groups: poor farmers, rich farmers, fishermen, nomads, farmers with livestock, casual labourers, full-time workers, artisans, factory workers, the destitute, the urban poor. Distinguish between the priorities of these groups and between men and women.

(continued over)

---

[2] In times of famine, child care practices are often the result of the previous two factors; for example, food insecurity may mean a shortage of adequate weaning foods, and so the mother is unable to wean her child properly. Alternatively, the limited coverage of the health services may mean the mother is unable to get her children vaccinated. Very often child care practices are restricted by the mother's access to resources.

112

Box 6.2   (cont.)

Resources
What types of resources are available? (Financial, organizational and human resources.) A shortage of organizational resources (civil and social administration, transport networks, health systems) severely hampers implementation. They may have been destroyed as a result of war or deteriorated to a state of collapse through long-term neglect. Additional financial resources may be needed to strengthen weak institutions and provide the necessary training and support for personnel.

Political context
What are the main political divisions? Who are the least-powerful groups or have least access to resources? Are any groups oppressed or discriminated against and if so, how and for what reason? How have these trends developed over recent years? What are the political sensitivities locally, nationally and internationally? Are any particular groups benefiting from the situation and if so how? At whom should programmes be targeted, or how can interventions be implemented so that the most vulnerable benefit?

page 13) to organize the main points (Box 6.2). The next section describes practical field methods for collecting relevant information.

Well-defined objectives and a clear idea of what you need to know help make sense of a sea of information. By contrast, if the objectives of the nutritional assessment are poorly defined, there may either be too much general information of no specific interest, or the minimum of anthropometric data which are impossible to interpret meaningfully.

Many more specific questions could be asked depending on the particular situation. An understanding of the normal seasonal patterns of disease and food security is vital for predicting future developments and their impact on health and nutrition.

With time, all situations change and produce different effects. This calls for a continuous system of assessment and analysis to monitor new developments.

What are the implications for methods of nutritional assessment?

Nutritional assessments, which combine a complementary mix of quantitative and qualitative methods, are a powerful tool for analysing both the causes and symptoms of famine and food security, and for achieving the objectives outlined earlier. The first objective is relatively straightforward and requires a quantitative estimate of anthropometric status and a comparison with previous estimates. For details of how to undertake an anthropometric survey see Chapter 3, pages 43–8.

The last three objectives are concerned with complex relationships and processes; malnutrition and its underlying causes; the effect of drought, war or similar misfortunes on different groups; the likelihood of food insecurity worsening; the potential health risks associated with malnutrition. For understanding causal relationships and underlying processes, qualitative methods are appropriate.[3] Rapid Rural Appraisal (RRA) is a flexible approach to gathering relevant and reliable information, which helps to identify local differences. Participatory Rural Appraisal (PRA) introduces the principles of community participation, which may be one of the main objectives of the assessment. A range of techniques can be adapted to suit the local circumstances.

The first stage of a nutritional assessment involves finding out about the normal seasonal patterns of nutritional status, food security and disease. This can often be achieved by reviewing 'secondary data' or existing information, such as previous survey reports.

Additional field-work should include anthropometric methods to determine nutritional status, semi-structured interviewing and other qualitative techniques to learn about underlying causes, and possibly a simple questionnaire to gain some additional quantitative data, say for example, about particular coping strategies that have been identified as being important.

The need for sentinel sites
The effects of seasonal stress and crises vary between different social and economic groups in the same environment. During the build up to a famine there is often great diversity in the effects of inadequate food security within an area and also between different groups dependent on different production systems. These complexities and subtleties are masked by data that are aggregated over a large area.

It is unwise to generalize about complex causal relationships among a diverse population or within a large area, as it can never be guaranteed that the same patterns hold in a different context. They may be similar, but often there are important differences that could radically affect the impact of drought and food security or the outcome of interventions.

For this reason, coverage of nutritional assessments of potential famine situations should be limited to small well-defined populations most of whom share certain characteristics, such as the basis of their livelihood (pastoral, agro-pastoral, agricultural, waged labour and so on). An overview of the wider situation is obtained by selecting several quite different 'sentinel' sites and making nutritional assessments at each location. Knowledge of which geographical or ecological regions or which population groups show persistently higher than average seasonal fluctuations in nutritional status, can contribute towards the selection of sentinel sites for routine surveillance.

---

[3] Reliable quantitative data are usually only available for a limited number of variables, so the number of associations between variables that can be tested statistically is quite limited.

Which nutritional index?

Weight-for-height is the most appropriate nutritional index for assessing short-term fluctuations in weight associated with recent changes in the diet or disease. This is especially useful for monitoring seasonal and unseasonal trends in nutritional status. It is unnecessary to determine the age of the children, which is time-consuming and difficult to establish accurately.

Arm circumference is also sensitive to short-term changes in weight, but the differences of MUAC observed between seasons and over the long term may be small compared to the level of measurement errors (Briend *et al.*, 1989a).

Implications for interpretation of nutritional data

Interpretation of results and reaching valid conclusions requires good judgement, which comes with understanding the processes at work and knowing what to look for and when. Before interpreting anthropometric results, check their reliability (Box 6.3).

Box 6.3   Tips for checking reliability and validity of anthropometric data

o Check the reliability of the methods used (sampling design, standard measurement techniques, reference values)

o Check for the possible confounding effect of migration or excess mortality.

o If comparisons are to be made of the same population over time, or of different populations, check that similar methods were used and that the age and sex distributions are similar. If not, adjust the data accordingly. Otherwise interpret results with extreme caution as the data sets are not comparable.

o If the main interest is the children at the lower end of the distribution, examine the proportion of children below the standard cut-off points for classifying weight-for-height (moderate <–2 SD scores, severe <–3 SD scores).

o If the main interest is changes in nutritional status, examine the mean nutritional status and the frequency distribution curve.

Interpretation of anthropometric data depends on the original objectives of the assessment and the other information collected. Review the results in the light of the questions posed in Box 6.2. Each situation must be examined independently, as sweeping generalizations usually hide important local differences.

Identify abnormal trends in nutritional status, diet composition, food security or disease, and identify the key underlying causes. Knowledge of seasonal patterns should suggest how the situation is likely to develop in the coming months. Even a very poor harvest may temporarily ease the problem of food shortages, although the situation will rapidly deteriorate once the meagre supplies have been used up. If there has been a drought,

115

the incidence of disease may have decreased, but is likely to increase sharply with the resumption of the rains.

Results must be interpreted in the context of the political situation which, particularly in the context of war and conflict, has a major impact on who is affected and why. An understanding of the political economy should help to identify the most politically vulnerable groups: those which are discriminated against and are defenceless in the face of oppression.

The conceptual framework (Figure 6.1) of nutritional status, malnutrition and death in famine, can assist in the interpretation of anthropometric data by helping to identify the stage of the famine process: is it an early stage when livelihoods are threatened, or a late stage when lives are at risk? This analysis is vitally important as it indicates the types of interventions that are appropriate.

An analysis of causes combined with a reliable measure of outcomes is a powerful combination for advocacy, as it provides an authoritative statement on what response is needed and why.

Box 6.4 Examples of intervention strategies at the early stage of famine intended to support livelihoods and improve access to food or income

Market interventions	General food subsidies. Management of food reserves to prevent fluctuating food prices. Subsidized weaning foods. Food tokens. Fair price shops.
Income support programmes	Employment schemes (food-for-work, cash-for-work on local construction projects: housing, roads, dams, wells, well protection, local amenities). Income-generating activities (production of useful local articles: rugs, mats, pottery). Exchange of livestock for cash, food or more drought-resistant animals. Direct cash support. Industrial projects (food processing: meat from de-stocking projects, production of weaning food or high-protein biscuits).
Agricultural support projects	Crop diversification and improvement (distribution of drought-resistant seeds and appropriate tools). Storage and transport. Marketing of produce. Horticulture, kitchen gardens.
Livestock support projects	Veterinary care. Fodder distribution. Water schemes.

Implications for interventions

Knowledge and understanding of the causes of high rates of malnutrition should help identify what actions are appropriate for dealing with the current problems. During the early stages of famine, following drought and a particularly severe hungry season, interventions should aim to support people's livelihoods, protect their entitlements and complement local efforts.

To sharpen the focus of the intervention, the local circumstances and potential must be well understood and defined. Knowledge of seasonal patterns of food security allows the particular problems posed by bad years to be predicted, which helps identify appropriate actions and the timing and targeting of these actions. Wage income opportunities are often seasonal in character, and so public works should be timed so as not to compete with regular work activities. Providing work during the slack agricultural period allows people to build up reserves for the coming hungry season when they they will need to work on their own farms.

Public health measures are vital to maintain health and prevent disease. During drought in the early stages of a famine public health may initially improve, and so the risk of death associated with high rates of malnutrition is reduced. However, with the resumption of the rains, conditions could rapidly deteriorate, intensifying exposure to disease and thereby aggravating the health risks of malnutrition.

Most famine deaths are an exaggeration of the normal seasonal patterns, so knowledge of these patterns and the current state of public health should indicate what measures need to be strengthened. These could include immunization coverage, access to essential drugs, clean water and sanitation, distribution of vitamin A, strengthening health outpost facilities and the training of health personnel. If food security improves, these measures will contribute to a more rapid recovery of nutritional status and general improvements in health. But if the situation fails to improve, the number of lives saved by these prompt actions is inestimable.

In the late stages of famine when lives are at risk, emergency relief takes priority. Direct interventions are needed to provide basic needs and prevent people from dying. These include shelter, food (including supplementary feeding), water, sanitation and curative health care. The risks to public health should determine what interventions should take priority.[4] Oxfam

---

[4] See: Centers for Disease Control. *Famine-affected, refugee, and displaced populations: recommendations for public health issues.* MMWR, 1992, 41 (No.RR-13), Available from; Superintendant of Documents, US Government Printing Office, Washington, D.C. 20402–9325.

has produced a series of practical guides which explain in detail how to organize the different aspects of an emergency relief programme.[5]

Implications for the role of food aid

> If food aid is a major resource at our disposal, we should seek ways of using it toward development of communities and betterment of the human condition, not just as another part of our medicine chest. George Beaton (ACC/SCN, 1992, page 52).

The role of food aid depends on the stage of the famine process and the objectives of the intervention. There is a big difference in approach between the use of food aid at an earlier stage of famine as an income/livelihood support, and the emergency use of food aid at a late stage of famine for providing an essential source of food and alleviating malnutrition. Food aid has a role to play in both objectives, but the way in which it is used differs markedly. The former takes into account people's priorities and involves some degree of people's participation. As a result, programmes are designed to fit in and complement the strategies of local people. By contrast, emergency interventions are by their very nature 'top-down' and assume a high degree of dependency of local people on outside assistance.

Because of these differences in approach, it is vital to ensure the correct timing of interventions, so that they coincide with the appropriate stage of famine. The argument used to justify the need for food aid is frequently based on saving lives, which is inappropriate at an early stage of famine. A mistimed emergency programme is simply a waste of everybody's time and resources, not to mention the potential damage such programmes do to the local economy and self-sufficiency. Sometimes emergency programmes begin after conditions are already improving, at which stage livelihood support measures would be more appropriate.

Use of food aid in the early stages of famine

In the earlier stages of famine when livelihoods are threatened, food aid has potentially a number of important roles, which are similar to the use of food aid for development (for examples of which see; ACC/SCN, 1992; Thomas *et al.*, 1989; Singer *et al.*, 1989). Food aid may serve directly as an

---

[5] Oxfam Practical Guide Series:
Selective Feeding Programmes, Lusty, T. and Diskett, P., 1984
Tuberculosis Control Programmes, Shears, P., 1988
Registration in Emergency Situations, Mitchell, J. and Slim, H., 1991
Food Scarcity and Famine, Young, H., 1992
Health Care for Refugees and Displaced People, Mears, C., and Chowdhury, S., 1994.
All titles available from the IT Publications Bookshop (for address, see back cover).

118

income or livelihood support measure, for example, food-for-work and de-stocking programmes. Food aid may be sold on the local market to generate local currency (counterpart funds[6]) to fund local projects (Box 6.4). Local reserves of food aid can serve to prevent sudden price fluctuations in local markets and ensure that supplies are available if emergency relief is called for.

The direct distribution of free food serves as an income transfer. The food aid releases income that would otherwise be spent on food or the food may be sold to generate income. In Red Sea Province, free food aid was provided by the World Food Programme and Oxfam to the Beja people between 1986 and 1989, as a means of economic recovery rather than as a source of essential nutrients (Mitchell *et al.*, 1990). In protracted (long-term) refugee situations the sale of food rations by refugees to buy other essentials is now commonplace, and is recognized as an acceptable practice by donors of food aid (Keen, 1992; USAID, 1988). The food aid commodities are rarely of high value and have a low resale value, especially when the market is flooded with food aid being sold by many refugees.

Use of food aid in the late stages of famine

In the late stages of famine, people who have been displaced from their homes are often entirely dependent on food assistance. Food rations usually consist of a limited number of basic food items; cereals, oil, beans and possibly a few other items. As the only source of food, the nutritional composition of food aid and food rations is critical. The limited number and types of foods means rations are frequently deficient in essential micronutrients, although it is possible to plan a balanced ration in terms of protein, fat and energy.

In practice, food distribution programmes are sometimes poorly organized and badly managed. Food supply and delivery problems are exacerbated by inappropriate methods of food distribution and registration. This results in late distribution of rations with items missing, and no rations at all for some groups. Suitable foods for weaning are rarely available in sufficient quantities. There are many cases where inadequate rations have contributed to protein energy malnutrition and outbreaks of micro-deficiency diseases, some of which (pellagra, scurvy, beriberi) have not been seen since the 1950s or even earlier.[7]

Apart from problems with the nutritional adequacy of the rations, there are additional problems of local milling of cereals and home preparation of food. Displaced people rarely have sufficient cooking equipment and water

---

[6] 'Monetization' of food aid is the disposal or sale of a certain percentage of food aid to pay for local administrative or transport expenses (Singer *et al.*, 1989).

[7] See the special issue on 'The Nutrition Crisis Among Refugees', *Journal of Refugee Studies*, Vol 5, No 3/4, 1992.

carriers. Cooking fuel can be an additional problem as large areas around relief camps are rapidly denuded of trees in the search of wood for fuel.

Selective feeding programmes are needed to target the particular nutritional needs of infants and young children, the malnourished and pregnant and lactating women. Special attention should be given to supporting breast-feeding mothers, and ensuring mothers have appropriate foods for weaning. In times of crisis, breast-feeding is often affected. The stress may contribute to feeding difficulites, or alternatively, because of inadequate weaning foods, mothers breast-feed for longer. Some, who have already weaned their infants, may revert to breast-feeding (Almedon, 1990).

Supplementary feeding programmes which are intended to alleviate malnutrition and thereby save lives are usually needed in the late stages of famine. During the early stages the objectives of feeding infants and young children are different. For example, a nursery combined with a supplementary feeding programme would benefit the nutrition of the individual child directly, and the food security of the household indirectly by freeing up the mother's time for earning income or producing food. This would be particularly appropriate during the agricultural season, when there is the greatest competition for the mother's time, and nutrition is under particular stress because of the hungry season. The organization and approach of such programmes should complement local strategies and any income/livelihood support measures.

Implications for targeting strategies

The purpose of targeting is to restrict the coverage of an intervention to those most in need—the most vulnerable. This maximizes the benefit of an intervention, while minimizing the costs involved. Alternatively, targeting has been used to match the number of programme participants with the available resources.

So who are the most vulnerable and how can they be identified? This depends on the objective of the intervention. Food aid in emergencies is usually targeted at the physiologically vulnerable: at those groups who are entirely dependent on outside food assistance, such as refugees, and those who are especially vulnerable, including the malnourished, infants, young children, pregnant and lactating women, the sick and elderly. But there are other types of vulnerability to be considered, including the food insecure and the politically vulnerable.

If the scope of intervention is broadened to address the causes of food insecurity and famine, the targeting strategies must identify the relevant vulnerable group, which might be a social or ethnic group rather than a physiologically vulnerable group.

Early stage of famine—targeting livelihood support measures
When the aim of intervention is to support people's livelihoods in order to avoid the worst effects of a bad season, interventions should be targeted at

the appropriate production systems. Those people engaged in vulnerable production systems may not necessarily be among the poorest members of a community whose production systems may have already collapsed. Consequently, the poor may be unable to take advantage of the opportunities made available by this type of intervention. To reach the poorest section of society, direct welfare or well-targeted income-generating activities may be needed.

Criteria for targeting individual poor households or particular production systems are usually based on either socio-economic criteria, local perceptions of need or self-selection (Box 6.5).

Within a community, anthropometric status of children is not a reliable proxy for either wealth or poverty of the family, as a child may be malnourished for different reasons. As our case-study in Part 2 showed, a child from a poor family is not necessarily malnourished, and a malnourished child is not necessarily from a poor family.

Geographic targeting of entire communities may be appropriate if most people have been similarly affected by food insecurity. Most villages are made up of several separate 'communities' or groups of people who are quite distinct from one another. These groups should be identified, and if possible, programmes targeted at the groups that need assistance. If targeting

---

Box 6.5   Targeting vulnerable production systems or poor households

Local knowledge and perceptions of need
In small cohesive communities, a local committee may nominate particular households according to their knowledge and perceptions of need. The success of this approach depends on the nature of local institutions and whether the poorer groups have a voice. Where the poor are powerless, the reliance on local institutions to allocate relief is problematic. In Darfur, the Red Crescent Committees were under pressure to extend the coverage of relief distribution to include most of the local population. This meant the proportion received by the poorest members of the community was smaller than if they had been targeted specifically.

Socio-economic criteria
In some circumstances a simple 'means' test is applied, based on indicators of need or poverty (location, asset ownership, landholdings/farm size, household age and sex structure). Decisions about appropriate criteria and cut-off points are largely a matter of local judgement, which is inevitably controversial and sometimes divides the community.

Self-selection
Targeting based on the principle of self-selection assumes that only the poor and destitute would volunteer themselves because of the social stigma and indignity of participating. For example, food-for-work programmes, or distribution of foods considered to be inferior.

is not possible, the programmes should be implemented so that all groups within the village benefit, and no single group is marginalized and therefore discriminated against.

Nutritional status of the community can serve as a good indicator of the food security situation. In conjunction with other information, anthropometric data can be used to confirm which locations are most food insecure. But in isolation anthropometric data should not be used to judge relative needs of different communities. Two villages with a similar rate of malnutrition may be facing entirely different circumstances, which are not apparent when looking at anthropometric data alone. Sentinel site surveillance restricts the use of nutritional status as a tool for community targeting as data are unavailable for all locations, and so few direct comparisons can be made.

Late stage of famine – targeting those at risk of dying

In the final stages of famine the priority is to save lives. Larger absolute numbers of infants and young children die in famine than any other age group. Because of the almost universal association between a decline in nutritional status and an increased risk of death, nutritional status is the best available indicator of those children with a higher risk of death. However, nutritional indices are not efficient at identifying *all* children at risk of dying. There is always some misclassification, as some children classified as malnourished do not die and many children above the cut-off point do in fact die.

Even though any nutritional status cut-off point excludes many children who die, it is not necessarily inefficient as an indicator of nutritional vulnerability. Well-nourished children die for reasons other than poor nutrition, which means that nutritional interventions intended to save lives do not necessarily need to be targeted at all children, but only at those with increased nutritional risk, that is, below the cut-off point. Other health-related interventions must obviously be targeted at all children to prevent them from becoming ill (immunization, vitamin-A distribution and so on).

If the prevalence of malnutrition is very high, or the mean nutritional status is very low, the most efficient strategy may be to include as many children as resources allow. This is particularly important in a poor health environment, in which increased exposure to disease is likely to have raised the threshold of nutritional status at which risk of death rises rapidly. In these situations moderate malnutrition as well as severe malnutrition may incur a high risk of death.

The resources saved by targeting fewer children (by reducing the cut-off point) may not justify missing many children who may eventually die. But on the other hand, the strategy of raising the nutritional status cut-off point in order to include more at-risk children may be prohibited by the additional costs of the intervention. Because of these difficulties, strategies for targeting individual at-risk children cannot be fixed. In practice, the targeting strategy must be decided according to the purpose of the intervention, local circumstances and the resources available.

Knowledge and understanding of the stage of the famine and the risks involved is necessary to work out solutions in the local context and to prevent the development of famine. But recent experience in Darfur and elsewhere suggests that good information is not sufficient to generate appropriate action or preventive measures. Early response has been more a matter of political incentives and motivation. This issue is reflected upon in the last chapter of the book.

CHAPTER 7

Community surveillance—lessons for the future

Introduction

Following the famine of 1984–5, the need for new approaches to nutritional surveillance was realized. Apart from the problem of inappropriate methods which did not suit the local circumstances or the needs of decision makers, there was a need to find an approach to surveillance which was feasible within the existing means and structures of Darfur. In the first years of the new programme there was great optimism as new links were forged with local communities. Much was learnt about the changing food security situation and its varying impact on different communities. This was achieved through purposive sampling and monitoring of sentinel sites, combining qualitative and quantitative methods and making community participation a key objective.

The involvement of the local people in Darfur in the collection of data, analysis and interpretation was an attempt to shift the locus of power away from technicians working in centralized offices, and towards the actual communities affected by food insecurity. The new approach tried to forge more equal relationships with both sides bringing their experience and expertise to the situation. A framework was developed to describe the nutritional status of the population and the underlying causes, which allowed local people to express their situation in terms understood by outsiders. This was important as the information was intended to be of practical use to decision makers at regional level as well as within the community.

There were many achievements over the three years of the case-study up to 1990. The participation of the community led to empowerment and strengthened the sustainability of the programme, and both outsiders and people from the community had a better understanding of nutrition and food security.

But community-based surveillance was not without its own particular problems and limitations. Many of these were linked, with a lack of all types of resources both within the community and at higher administrative levels. The public service infrastructure was extremely weak, and there were few trained and experienced personnel. This affected the scaling-up of the programme to cover a wider area and meant that only limited support was available for community-based initiatives.

The strengths of community-based surveillance

Sentinel sites give a sharper focus

The sentinel site approach succeeded in sharpening the focus of nutritional assessments and provided relevant information that prompted an immediate response to the problem of malnutrition, and more long-term initiatives to support vulnerable livelihoods.

In-depth assessments of smaller areas in the more food insecure northeast of Darfur showed huge seasonal variations in food security and nutritional status, and important differences between the food security of adjacent villages. These communities showed early changes in nutritional status in response to a worsening food security situation. The impact of confounding variables was easier to check, and subtle differences between social and ethnic groups were more readily apparent. These results were in direct contrast to region-wide surveys which combined data from many diverse areas and averaged out local differences. For decision makers, these 'average' figures are little more than blunt instruments as they give no indication of who or where is most affected or why.

The limited coverage of each assessment allowed the analysis of anthropometric data to be done in the village, so assessment reports could be made available very soon after the field-work (unlike the long delays experienced with the centralized analysis of large-scale survey results).

Improved validity of information

The combination of qualitative and quantitative methods greatly enhanced the validity and reliability of results. Both approaches have their own particular strengths and weaknesses, but used in combination, they each compensate for the limitations of the other approach (Chapter 3, page 58).

Quantitative data usually only describe a problem, and give limited insights into the causes of malnutrition and the likelihood of future improvement or decline.[1] In contrast, qualitative methods are able to reveal complex underlying relationships, like the impact of seasonal changes in food security on nutritional status. Qualitative methods are invaluable for learning about local differences and change. But qualitative data are sometimes perceived as being unreliable and too subjective because of the influence of field-workers, who bring their experience, values and behaviourial style to the situation and the results. This subjectivity is countered to some extent by including some quantitative measures, say for example, anthropometric assessments, which are designed to maximize reliability.

---

[1] Causal analysis using quantitative data is generally impractical, as it requires large sample sizes and detailed household questionnaires that cover all potential causal factors.

In Darfur, qualitative methods helped identify quantitative indicators which were potentially useful for early warning of famine, for example, the proportion of households eating wild foods (especially *mukheit*), or who had fresh milk available. As food security deteriorated following a series of poor harvests, the proportion of households eating wild foods gradually increased from year to year (Figure 5.2). The proportion of households consuming *mukheit* gradually crept upwards from 9.4 per cent in July 1989, to 82.2 per cent in January 1991, unlike malnutrition which despite the worsening situation did not exceed 40 per cent during the three years of the case-study.

The validity of conclusions and recommendations can be improved by the participation of people from the local community. The active involvement of local people in both the nutritional assessments and community surveillance helped to ensure that outsiders did not misunderstand their situation, and indicated their views and priorities.

Participation and empowerment

In Darfur, the degree of participation changed and developed during the course of the case-study. Initially, participation was limited to co-opting local people to help out with collecting information and to contribute their views and opinions. Later, participation as a means of empowerment became one of the underlying principles of community-based surveillance. Community leaders and representatives were consulted as to whether they wanted to organize and operate their own surveillance system.

A subsequent evaluation of the programme found out why they agreed to participate (Ojaba and Abduljabbar, 1992). Principally, they believed it would improve the lot of their community, to which they had a powerful sense of social obligation and commitment. From their previous experience of famine relief they were convinced that information presented on paper in terms well understood by the government and donor agencies would receive more attention than their verbal complaints. Hence, empowerment of the community as a group to seek support and demand their share of available resources was a strong motivation. Connected with this was the prestige and social recognition of participating in the programme. On the other hand, they were aware that it would help them find out what was happening in their areas, which could help them find their own solutions.

These reasons were enough to ensure the continued participation of the community, even during those difficult years when no food aid or other assistance was available. According to Ojaba and Abduljabbar:

> The benefits of the programme to the communities as a group were the strengthening of the communities' capabilities of being able to monitor and appraise the food security situation in their areas, and being able to identify ways to remedy some of their problems by themselves or through assistance from external sources (page 20).

Local solutions were sought, and the community representatives through the local Red Crescent Committees actively assisted individual food insecure families. For example, they sold food commodities at cost price, which forced local merchants to lower their prices, and organized a supplementary feeding programme with locally collected funds.

A more sustainable approach

From the beginning it was realized that surveillance activities could only be sustained if they were well within the means of local institutions in Darfur. Otherwise, if donor funds were withdrawn, the programme would collapse. This was one reason why large-scale region-wide surveys were rejected, as previously in Sudan they had soaked up huge amounts of donor funds to pay for vehicles, fuel, staff salaries and field expenses. Field-work also took valuable staff away from their main jobs for long periods. The sentinel site approach and rapid assessments were designed to minimize costs and so promote long-term sustainability.

In a rapidly changing political climate, community monitoring was far less affected than projects directly implemented by government and agencies, and undoubtedly community participation contributed to the lasting sustainability of the programme. During the case-study years there was a rapidly changing political climate, as changes in government lead to frequent changes in the directorate of the Darfur Ministry of Health, and the withdrawal of donor funds led to the departure of several NGOs. Their programmes were directly affected and many collapsed or temporarily ceased to function.

The limitations of community-based surveillance

Coverage and scaling-up

The key problem of sentinel site surveillance coupled with community participation was coverage. Trade-offs had to be made between depth of understanding of individual communities and the number of communities covered. Scaling-up is not just a matter of more financial resources, as the success of community surveillance lies in developing good working relationships between insiders and outsiders.

Local people can be trained in the correct anthropometric procedures, but they continue to need support once the programme has been established. The use of qualitative methods requires more training than simple questionnaire surveys as it requires a broad understanding of nutrition and food security, which is necessary in deciding what information is relevant. There are few 'experts' available who are experienced in qualitative methods and a participatory approach who are able to pass on these skills to others.

Scaling-up from a few sentinel sites to a wider coverage of Darfur was impractical in the short-term. It required additional financial and human resources and even then would have taken a long time to achieve.

Costs to the community

There was also a considerable cost to the community, which had to maintain the monitoring irrespective of whether it was a good or bad year. In Darfur, a great deal was expected of the monitors, who had to measure the random sample of children every three months. In addition, they had to interpret the results in the light of the qualitative information and consider possible solutions. This is a tall order, even for most trained and experienced nutritionists, and far exceeds the expectations placed on fieldworkers by traditional nutrition survey methods.

All the monitors were volunteers who received no remuneration for their monitoring work which had to fit in with their other commitments. The monitors faced problems not encountered by the rapid assessment teams. They were less mobile and the children to be measured were scattered. Also, because the monitors were local, people were less conscientious about attending on the appointed day.

Even in good years, maintaining nutrition monitoring has its own particular problems, as weighing and measuring is a much more intrusive monitoring technique than, for example, interviewing. It also involves many families, who may find the regular commitment time-consuming and inconvenient. The motivation to participate must come from an understanding of the wider aims of the programme, as there are no immediate benefits to the children or their family or to the monitors.

Dependency on outsiders

Self-help initiatives by the community were severely restricted by a lack of local resources and the inadequacy of the public service infrastructure. Many government services, particularly health, were either non-existent or unsupportive, which hampered the efforts of the community. During one particularly difficult period, the Red Crescent committee and local medical assistant raised local funds to organize supplementary feeding for the malnourished children, but the scale of the need soon exhausted the locally available funds, which were not supplemented by additional external resources.

A response from government and agencies was never guaranteed and could not be relied upon. Initially the donors looked favourably on North Darfur, and in 1988 the Western relief operation was intended to prevent a famine. But later political events in Sudan in 1989 and 1990 shaped donor policy, and several key donors withdrew all development aid and were only willing to provide humanitarian aid. Humanitarian aid can only be justified in the very late stages of famine or other food-related crisis, when people are destitute and lives are at risk. Humanitarian aid cannot be used to justify an early set of more appropriate interventions aimed at supporting vulnerable livelihoods.

Information collected by local people carries less authority and has a lower credibility than the apparently sophisticated surveys of outsiders. This reduces its value for advocacy. In June and July, 1991, the nutrition monitors carried out an assessment and weighed and measured all children. The results showed high rates of malnutrition, which fitted in with previous patterns. But the authorities in Khartoum questioned the reliability of such community monitoring, which provided a convenient excuse to ignore the data.

Participation—rhetoric and reality!

Participation in nutritional surveillance is inevitably restricted by the technical aspects of data collection and analysis imposed upon the community from outside. Measurement of anthropometric status and random sampling are both difficult concepts to understand. Standard procedures are endorsed by experts, and there are many rules about their application. The use of these techniques hardly seems very participatory. However, the community supported the idea of measuring anthropometric status as they considered it to be a reliable measure of one aspect of their food insecurity.

People involved in the longitudinal-monitoring programme initially thought malnutrition was more common in poorer households, which influenced their attitudes to sampling. In one community the monitors preferred to measure all children in order to ensure that all the poor households were included, while in another village there was reluctance to include the richer households in the random sample. In both cases, people found the idea of a representative random sample difficult to understand, and thought it unlikely to represent adequately the problems of the poor.

Despite considerable success in generating a participatory approach to surveillance, the most active roles tended to be taken up by community representatives and members of the local Red Crescent committees who were better off than most people in the area. They did not participate because they stood to gain directly, rather they felt responsible towards their communities. There was a degree of social recognition and prestige involved.

But despite these worthy aims, they did not extend the principles of active participation within the community to involve mothers, the poor and dispossessed (Ojaba and Abduljabbar, 1992). Discussions about survey results tended to be shared between the monitors and key community figures, which denied access to the majority of the community. Mothers in particular were not given an opportunity to benefit from the knowledge

129

gained. Clearly, participation by community representatives on behalf of the community is not enough, and all concerned groups must be consulted and given the opportunity to participate fully.

North Darfur after 1990

As a result of political events in 1989 and 1990, key donors to Darfur withdrew their support, and funding of long-term development programmes ceased. This led to the collapse of the Agricultural Planning Unit, which co-ordinated the food information system, and later the collapse of the drought monitoring programme of the Sudanese Red Crescent. Within a short period of time the entire early warning system in Darfur ceased to exist, with the one exception of the community-based nutritional surveillance programme which continued to collect data and file reports to El Fasher.

The lack of external assistance to the sentinel site villages following the serious decline in nutrition and food security in 1990 threatened the sustainability of community participation. The closer relationship between these communities and regional authorities had produced little support of community initiatives. There were no immediate benefits to the community, and few incentives to continue the monitoring. Also, as food security worsened, the livelihoods of the monitors themselves were in jeopardy, and some in fact left the area. Even the Oxfam field-workers were reluctant to visit the areas if they were to find a worsening nutritional situation when there was no possibility of a response. To cope with this difficult situation, it was decided to expand the coverage of household assessments and limit the anthropometric measurements.

Changing circumstances and changing uses of the data

Originally one of the main uses of information collected by community surveillance was to complement the broader indicators monitored by the region-wide early warning system (rainfall, agriculture, market prices). But by 1990, the use of the surveillance information at a regional level changed. The region's food information system collapsed because of the withdrawal of external support from the Agricultural Planning Unit. As the only remaining component of the early warning system there was great pressure on the nutritional surveillance system to provide information over a wider area, which it was unable to do while still maintaining the same participatory approach. In the absence of the wider information system, the reports of the community surveillance programme were inadequate for the needs of national-level planners, as information from sentinel sites was largely irrelevant to national-level decision makers who wished to make comparisons of the nutritional situation in different regions in Sudan.

Back to where we started

Once more centralized relief planning took over, and donor funds were made available to the Ministry of Health in Khartoum to implement large-scale nutrition surveys in the worst-affected regions of north Sudan (Darfur, Kordofan and Red Sea Hills initially). This was against the advice of the Darfur Ministry of Health who supported the community-based nutritional surveillance programme. History repeated itself; the large-scale surveys took several months to complete and encountered the same old problems of inadequate sampling frame, inaccessible areas, lack of analysis of the food security situation or who was affected. Survey reports from all regions gave the same bland general recommendations, and thus failed to recognize the complex differences within and between the regions. However, they were successful in confirming that prevalence rates of wasting had been alarmingly high, probably as a result of the poor food security situation. But because of the time delays in reporting this information, it was somewhat academic, and even the role of information for advocacy was minimal.

In 1991 Save the Children Fund started its relief-monitoring activities and collected both socio-economic and nutritional information, mainly for the purposes of monitoring its relief operations. They made use of the household questionnaires developed for the rapid nutritional assessments, and adopted the sentinel site approach. But the expanded coverage meant they ended up with so much information they had difficulties analysing it. Eventually they employed an expatriate specifically for this purpose, but the results were available too late to be of much practical use.

In 1992 SCF started producing regular food and nutrition bulletins, which presented food security related information on the socio-economic, nutritional and health situation in five of the area councils in North Darfur. The information was used mostly for advocacy, and in some cases for targeting food aid, in particular supplementary foods (Unimix).

That same year Oxfam agreed to postpone the community-based surveillance monitoring activities in Malha, Mareiga and Cuma as SCF wanted to include these areas in its relief-monitoring programme. Apart from some additional information on health aspects, SCF adopted a similar survey methodology as used by Oxfam.

In October 1993 SCF changed the nutritional surveillance methodology from sentinel site surveillance back to random selection of villages; this time 105 villages were sampled. They recognized that this region-wide approach is clearly unsustainable, but feel they need to be more 'thorough' in their assessments of the scale of intervention needed. This is particularly important both as there were questions about whether the scale of the SCF programme in 1993 had been necessary, and for planning interventions in the future (Blewitt, personal comm., 1994).

Why were the lessons learnt so quickly forgotten?

Many lessons had been learnt from the experience of assessments of famine situations in the mid-eighties and earlier, yet by the early nineties it seemed that many had already been forgotten. Events from 1991 to 1993 could easily have been a re-run of a decade earlier, as outside agencies such as UNICEF and Save the Children spent large sums of donor funds on grand nutritional surveillance programmes unsuited to conditions in Darfur. Sooner or later this might be realized, in which case we expect that following the current relief programme there will be a search for more sustainable solutions and appropriate methodologies!

There are many possible reasons why the lessons learnt after the 1984–5 famine were no longer applied after 1990. Some have already been mentioned, such as the changing circumstances in Darfur which affected the objectives of nutritional surveillance. There was pressure from national-level organizations for 'hard' data for the purposes of advocacy and mounting appeals for resources. This took precedence over other more local information needs, and the goal of community participation was considered to be less important.

The international staff involved also had a major impact. They are usually employed on short-term contracts, and have little time to familiarize themselves with the area, let alone what happened in previous relief operations. In Darfur, one of the key technical experts who contributed towards the design of the current programme admitted they knew nothing of the regional information system developed after the 1984–5 famine when the new programme was initiated in 1991. Field-workers are restricted in their approach by the pressing need for information from their head offices, who want so-called 'hard' data. There are also few personnel who are familiar with a broader range of methods, such as sentinel site surveillance and rapid rural appraisal techniques.

Resources are rarely available for 'alternative' approaches, yet vast sums are regularly spent on massive surveys that produce no tangible benefits. It could be argued that high-cost intensive surveillance systems are justified alongside large scale-relief operations, particularly in the absence of other information. However, large-scale relief operations are usually short term, and this type of surveillance system cannot be sustained without large external funds. The costs of withdrawing and re-establishing a programme are likely to be higher than maintaining a continuous small-scale presence.

At the height of a relief operation there is little room for new approaches, and there is not the time to develop a truly participatory approach. But between emergencies there is the time and opportunity to remove the blinkers and be more innovative! Only then can we hope to develop sustainable systems adapted to the huge constraints in an area like Darfur.

CHAPTER 8

A role for nutrition—practical or pointless?

The discipline of nutrition as it is currently applied is rapidly becoming irrelevant to the nutritional problems of famine-affected populations and refugees. Problems of inadequate nutrition are escalating, especially in Africa where unprecedented numbers of displaced people and refugees are now dependent on international relief.

The role of the nutritionist has been marginalized and is frequently little more than to undertake anthropometric assessments and supervise supplementary feeding programmes. These temporary measures, and tunnel vision, have side-tracked nutritionists who have had minimal impact on the causes of malnutrition and thus have not succeeded in raising nutritional status in the longer term.

We have been seduced by anthropometry, which is easy to measure, easy to manipulate and can be easily taken out of context to mean just about anything! This has stunted our analytical skills, and created a strait-jacketed approach to famine relief; high rates of malnutrition equal famine equal food distribution. So nutritionists frequently fail at this first task of assessment, as they focus their efforts on what can be measured, that is, anthropometry, rather than taking a broader and deeper view of nutritional problems and their solutions.

Why has this happened, when surely nutritionists have so much more to contribute? We believe we have lost sight of our goals, which have been reduced to little more than maximizing the statistical reliability of our anthropometric estimates and counting calories. This is partly a result of pressure from employers; those agencies and institutions who recruit nutritionists on short-term contracts, and are themselves under pressure to use nutritional information to mount effective appeals to secure funding. It is also partly our own fault: get a group of nutritionists together and what do they discuss? The relative merits of arm circumference and weight-for-height or other technical details, not, 'How do we address nutritional problems more effectively?'

Other important reasons for the increasing irrelevance of nutrition to famine-affected and refugee populations rest with the humanitarian aid policies and mandates of donors and agencies, and the difficulties of resourcing new initiatives. In concluding this book we consider some of the pre-conditions required to ensure a more effective combined attack on the nutritional problems of our times.

Nutritionists of the future

There is a need to broaden the role of nutritionists, first in assessments and analysis of a situation, and second in finding solutions suited to the local context. In terms of assessments, nutritionists should contribute a wider understanding of the underlying causes of malnutrition and food insecurity, and be able to analyse the basic causes or at the very least be aware of them. This should include an analysis of the availability of all types of resources (economic, human and organizational) at the appropriate administrative levels, within the local political context.

This requires specific training and education, which are included in few current courses on nutrition. Courses must expand their teaching from the application of technical blueprints, to include an understanding of the diversity of experience of famine, war and oppression, and an understanding of the practical constraints of implementation. Nutritionists need to have a basic conceptual understanding of the processes at work.

The inappropriate training of nutritionists was a key issue identified by Alan Berg as contributing towards 'our failure to make larger dents in malnutrition' or as he termed it 'nutrition malpractice' (Berg, 1991). He suggests we need 'nutrition engineers'; nutritionists who know about the nuts and bolts of implementation. That means in addition to nutrition, students need to be trained in economics, administration, logistics, planning and budgeting as well as the other necessary skills for effective implementation of programmes. Personnel must have both managerial and analytical skills.

A participatory approach to learning is vital, to take into account the practical experience of staff from governments, donors and agencies, including field-workers. By participating in courses, these experienced people would actively contribute to the learning process. Greater attention must be given to learning about the views and perspectives of victims of famine, who affect the success or failure of interventions by outsiders. In the rush of mounting an international relief operation, the rights of ordinary people to be consulted about decisions that affect their lives is often overlooked.

Expanding the relief mandate and resourcing new initiatives

A simple distinction can be drawn between humanitarian aid for emergencies, and longer-term development aid, which must cover the rest of the spectrum from development, through prevention and mitigation, to rehabilitation once the emergency is over. Humanitarian aid programmes usually provide no more than a temporary 'band aid', which can have unfortunate long-term effects as they act as a disincentive to local production and lead to longer-term impoverishment.

In Africa, humanitarian aid is rising rapidly, while development assistance is either stagnant or in decline (Duffield, 1994). During the early eighties, the total emergency spending by the UK's Overseas Development Administration, for example, was between 2–3 per cent of the total UK aid programme. By 1991–2 it had increased to 11 per cent, about two-thirds of which being directed through the UN and NGOs (Duffield, 1994). UNI-CEF's expenditure on emergencies increased by nearly 350 per cent to $167 million between 1989 and 1992 (Duffield, 1994).

Criteria of good governance have been used to withhold development aid, as for example, in Kenya, Malawi and Sudan. This has led to the collapse of many long-term development programmes, while short-term funding of humanitarian relief becomes the only form of international support. Some believe that relief systems are a symptom of the Western countries' disengagement with the South (Pallister, 1994).

Despite the ever-increasing amounts spent on humanitarian aid, there are great uncertainties and inconsistencies in the international response to emergencies. Priorities have become confused. The international response to emergencies tends to be dictated by political attitudes, the availability of funding, and the attention of the world's media, rather than any objective assessment of need. Emergency appeals are seldom if ever met in full. In relation to the 26 complex emergencies supported by the UN in 1993, on average 57 per cent of the appeal was being received (UN, 1993, cited by Duffield, 1994).

The most severe famines have been associated with war and conflict, and the climate of humanitarian relief has changed as a result. Agencies like Oxfam and Médecins Sans Frontières have regularly spoken out against atrocities and used the media to press the case for intervention to relieve civilian suffering in war zones.

The UN's humanitarian role has changed dramatically as it has increasingly intervened in the domestic affairs of a state. In April 1991, Security Council resolution 688 condemned Iraq for its treatment of the civilian population and set up safe havens with an air exclusion zone. This was followed by resolution 770 which provided UN military protection for humanitarian convoys in Bosnia. Then came resolution 794 which authorized UN troops to use 'all necessary means' in Somalia to secure the unimpeded distribution of aid, and finally, the authorization of NATO close support air strikes against the Serbs (Pallister, 1994). These interventions in the domestic affairs of a state have raised the political importance of humanitarian aid.

The mandate of relief agencies has been expanded, UNHCR for example, was originally responsible for assisting those who crossed international borders. But their work has now been extended in some cases to include long-term refugees, returnees, the local population and the internally displaced. This is decided on a case-by-case basis, so assistance to the internally displaced is by no means automatic. In Somalia and Kenya UNHCR proposed the creation of buffer zones in which all UN agencies and NGOs work together as a strong co-ordinated team, and harmonize activities on both

135

sides of the border between Kenya and Somalia. In Somalia under established offices in the areas of origin of refugees in Kenya, the aim was to prevent a further exodus of refugees, and encourage repatriation. A community-based approach was taken, with priority being given to essential development activities such as water supply, primary health care, education, livestock and veterinary services and agriculture. This marks a radical change from UNHCR's usual assistance programme for refugees.

But despite these developments the focus of humanitarian aid is still the peak of the emergency when lives have already been lost, and for many victims it is too late to avert the catastrophic effects. Relief is limited to providing the basic essentials of food, water, shelter and so on, and does little or nothing to protect people's livelihoods and assure them a viable future.

The mandate of relief agencies must be broadened to include an earlier response to the effects of famine and food insecurity aimed at reducing vulnerability and supporting livelihoods. These initiatives would apply equally in protracted emergencies in which people are unable to resume their previous way of life but must develop alternative livelihoods.

At present, funds for early interventions, such as livelihood support measures, cannot be justified as humanitarian relief because, to put it simply, lives are not at risk and it is too soon to be predicting the biggest and worst-ever disaster. There appears to be a clear donor preference to fund only immediate relief needs, and then only once suffering and dislocation have reached intolerable proportions (Duffield, 1994). Early interventions also do not qualify for support under longer-term development programmes, as funds are normally committed well in advance, and are tied to specific longer-term programmes. Early warning systems do not have funds earmarked for responding to early signs of a decline in food security. So it seems the very initiatives needed to prevent the situation from worsening, very often cannot be supported, as few if any relief agencies have the mandate or expertise to support an earlier set of more appropriate community-level interventions. Even if they had, from whom or where would they find the means?

There is competition for resources on all sides; agencies with a relief mandate compete with development agencies. Most relief agencies have few resources to allow them to act at once, but must launch appeals to donors based on their most recent needs assessments or early warning information. Voluntary agencies often compete with each other for funds from the same citizenry and also from donors. Several UN agencies have a mandate to undertake emergency relief including WFP, UNHCR, UNDP, FAO, WHO, UNDRO and UNICEF and they often launch separate appeals and compete for the same donor funds.

The pool of international funds is already inadequate, and these latest developments in humanitarian assistance take up ever-increasing amounts of resources. In the face of a human tragedy, urgent solutions are called for, but they should not be at the expense of sustainable development programmes which protect the vulnerable and neutralize the threat of famine.

An overview of the nutritional surveillance methods used in North Darfur 1988–91

Methods for rapid nutrition assessments

A combination of quantitative and qualitative methods were used. Speed in reporting results was considered essential, which meant visiting only a limited number of individual communities, but allowing more time in each. This was intended to give a deeper, more insightful understanding of the impact of the harvest on food security and nutrition and how people were managing to survive. A further priority was spending more time with people; at least one night and usually longer was spent in each village, listening and talking, in order to learn about perceptions of food security and nutritional problems.

Selection of village councils to survey
Those village councils most affected by food insecurity were selected. For example, in the first survey in 1988 five villages in Umm Keddada area council were visited; three villages which had previously been included in the pre-harvest survey and which were considered by the APU to be representative of the area as a whole were selected, and so were two villages that were reported to be suffering severe hardship.

Quantitative methods for rapid nutrition assessments
In each village all children over 65cm in length and under 115cm were weighed to the nearest 0.1kg and their height was measured to the nearest 0.5cm by the survey team assisted by local volunteers using standard procedures (WHO, 1983). The child's minder was also asked the sex and age of the child, number of siblings and obvious symptoms of disease (diarrhoea, cough, fever or vomiting) experienced during the past two weeks. Morbidity was dropped from the anthropometric survey forms in 1989 because information about disease was obtained from the local health worker.

Sometimes separate formal questionnaires were completed with the mother's help on a range of topics depending on the particular assessment, for example:

○ The main occupation of household members and wages earned.
○ Other sources of income, particularly during the dry season (trading of handicrafts, building materials, fuel).

137

- ○ Location and activities of absent family members (labour migration).
- ○ Source of millet or sorghum (own production, local or distant markets, receipt of food aid, purchase of subsidized relief grain).
- ○ Household consumption of fresh milk, wild foods and bread.

Questions were not asked about household assets (income, livestock, etc.), as answers were difficult to validate and the sensitivity of the questions may have jeopardized the developing relationship between field-workers and the community.

As knowledge about any one area grew, questions became more specific about food security issues in the area. After the questionnaires were completed, there was usually time for a more relaxed discussion of points of interest.

Qualitative information for rapid nutrition assessments
On arrival, the team met with the local leaders: the local council officials and the traditional leaders (Sheikh or Omda). Following the appropriate introductions, the team leader explained the purpose of the visit and together with the local leaders drew up a rough timetable for the stay and enlisted volunteers.

Unstructured interviews and informal discussions were held with various groups and individuals in the village. Key informants with a specialist knowledge of the village included for example, the medical assistant, midwife, teachers or members of the local SRC committee. Following the interviews with key informants, additional questions were sometimes added to the household questionnaires, for which space on the forms had been allowed. There were many other *ad hoc* talks with local people during visits to people's homes, the marketplace, the mill, the well or water pump and outlying farms.

Some interviews were semi-structured using previously drawn up check lists, which included the main topics of interest, for example, water supply, population movements, the agricultural and livestock situation and availability of grain and wild foods. Many important talks and discussions happened spontaneously.

This approach provided a rapid assessment of the food and nutrition situation, and allowed time to start a dialogue and get to know local people better.

One other technique deserving a special mention is wealth ranking which is a powerful means of finding out about local perceptions of wealth and differences in wealth within the community. Wealth ranking was first used by the rapid assessment team in 1988 to evaluate a targeted food distribution programme. The families of those children whose anthropometric status was less than 80 per cent weight-for-height were wealth ranked.

Wealth ranking was used again by the team in 1989 to obtain information on the wealth status of families that had been selected for regular monitoring.

(For further information on wealth-ranking see Grandin 1988, *Wealth-ranking in Smallholder Communities: A field manual*, IT Publications.)

Analyses, interpretation and report writing

The anthropometric status of individual children was calculated in the village. The prevalence of wasting and average anthropometric status was then discussed with local leaders or representatives. The intention was to learn their views about the underlying causes and discuss potential solutions.

Reports from the rapid nutrition assessments were written in English usually within one week or sometimes two weeks of the field-work. Much of the information confirmed the results of the pre-harvest surveys and other reports, but gave more detail about specific aspects of food security in particular villages or among certain groups. Recommendations for interventions were included if they had been previously discussed and agreed upon with local representatives. The reports were distributed among agencies, ministries and donors within Darfur and Khartoum. An Arabic translation of the summary was sent to the local authorities in the areas surveyed.

Methods for longitudinal monitoring

After the good harvest of 1988, the need for rapid assessments in food insecure areas was reduced and there was time to develop a regular community monitoring system. The emphasis was on monitoring by the community, rather than by outsiders.

Malha, Mareiga and Cuma towns were selected as sentinel sites for regular nutritional monitoring. They had hardly recovered from the 1984–5 famine, when they were badly hit by the effects of harvest failure in 1987. As a result they had been included in the rapid nutrition assessments, which confirmed that these towns were extremely vulnerable to food insecurity. The anthropometric status of these communities was expected to show the first signs of additional stress caused by a deterioration in food security. Regular monitoring would therefore strengthen the regional early warning system.

Apart from the early warning role of anthropometric data, it was hoped that both Oxfam's and the community's understanding of nutritional problems would improve.

Unlike many development projects, the community did not stand to gain any tangible benefits other than information. Oxfam made it clear from the beginning that one of the objectives was to provide regular information to the regional information system of the Agricultural Planning Unit, partly for early warning, and partly to gain a better understanding of nutritional problems and to identify possible solutions. But there were no resources set aside to fund any community-based proposals. The proposed monitoring programme was discussed at length with village leaders, who had already experienced several nutritional surveys and knew what they might expect. But with the assurance that this programme was to be different, because of the involvement of the community, they agreed to participate.

Community monitoring encouraged the development of much closer relationships between local communities, local government and agencies. This also helped address the problem of non-participation and survey fatigue, as people had the opportunity of discussing the relevance of the results and so were more interested in the programme. The low cost of community monitoring was also thought to increase the chances of long-term sustainability.

The community monitors
Community leaders identified three volunteers, two women and one man, to be trained as community monitors. A short course covered basic nutrition concepts and simple survey procedures. The aim was to train them not only how to weigh and measure children, but also how to analyse and interpret the results. This was achieved by raising awareness of the underlying causes of malnutrition which might be present in their communities. For example, water supply, agriculture, livestock, markets and outbreaks of disease. The seasonal patterns of nutrition were also discussed.

Quantitative methods for longitudinal monitoring
Fifty households were randomly selected from a sampling frame of all children in the community, which had been drawn up during census surveys in 1988 and early 1989. The children from the 50 families were weighed and measured as in the rapid nutrition assessments. The monitors calculated the anthropometric status of each child, using a calculator and weight-for-height tables, and then calculated the prevalence below 80 per cent weight-for-height.

Additional information was collected in separate interviews with mothers. In the first round of monitoring, the interviews recorded details about the child and its family (age, sex, number of siblings, main occupation of head of household). In subsequent rounds of monitoring, the interview was reduced to three topics: source of millet or sorghum, and consumption of fresh milk and wild foods. These variables were expected to change over time, whereas information on other topics was expected to change less frequently.

The selected families were monitored every three to four months, for a period of one year. After one year, a census survey of all children in the community was carried out, from which a new sample of 50 families was chosen to be monitored the following year.

Qualitative information for longitudinal monitoring
The local monitors used a check-list to collect information on the underlying causes of malnutrition. The gravity of the prevalence of malnutrition

140

was discussed by the monitors in the light of this additional qualitative information, and the information from interviews with mothers.

Report writing
The monitors summarized the results of monitoring, including the prevalence of malnutrition, results of the household interviews, a summary of the qualitative information on the underlying causes of malnutrition, and finally their view or interpretation of the nutritional situation. These summary sheets were sent to El Fasher, together with the raw data.

The summary was translated into English and the anthropometric data were typed into a computer file to allow its conversion into Z scores. Standardized reports on each round of monitoring were disseminated to agencies, ministries and donors in Darfur and Khartoum.

REFERENCES

ACC/SCN, 1992, 'Nutritional Issues in Food Aid', ACC/SCN Symposium Report, Nutrition Policy Discussion Paper No 12, ACC/SCN, Geneva.

Adams, M.E. and Hawksley, E., 1989, 'Merging relief and development: The case of Darfur', *Development Policy Review*, 7: 143–169.

Alam, N., Wojtyniak, B., Rahaman, M.M., 1989, 'Anthropometric indicators and risk of death', *American Journal of Clinical Nutrition*, 49: 884–8.

Almedon, A., 1990, Child weaning practices in times of crisis, RPN, No 9: 24–26.

Andersson, N., Martinez, E., Cerrato, F., Morales, E., Ledogar, R., 1989, 'The use of community based data in health planning in Mexico and Central America', *Health Policy and Planning*, 3 (3): 197–206

Arnauld, J., Alarcon, J.A., Imink, M.D.C., 1990, 'Food security and food and nutritional surveillance in Central America: The need for functional approaches', *Food and Nutrition Bulletin* 12 (1).

Autier, P., D'Altilia, J.P., Delamalle, J.P., Vercruysse, V., 1989, 'The food and nutrition surveillance systems of Chad and Mali: The SAP after two years', *Disasters*, 13 (1).

Bairagi, R., 1987, 'A comparison of five anthropometric indices for identifying factors of malnutrition', *American Journal of Epidemiology*, 126, 2: 258.

Bairagi, R., Chowdhury, M.K., Kim, Y.J., Curlin, G.T., 1985, 'Alternative anthropometric indicators of mortality', *American Journal of Clinical Nutrition*, 42: 296–306.

Beaton, G., Kelly, A., Kevary, J., Martorell, R., Mason, J., 1990, 'Appropriate uses of anthropometric indices in children', A report based on an ACC/SCN workshop. ACC/SCN State of the Art Series Nutrition Policy Discussion Paper No 7, ACC/SCN, Geneva.

Beaton, G.H., Martorell, R., Aronson, K.J., Edmonston, B., McCabe, G., Ross, A.C., Harvey, B., 1993, 'Effectiveness of vitamin A supplementation in the control of young child morbidity and mortality in developing countries', ACC/SCN State of the Art Series, Nutrition Policy Discussion Paper No 13, Geneva.

Bedreldin Shutta, 1993, 'Nutritional surveillance programme, Final report', mimeo, Oxfam Darfur, western Sudan.

Berg, A., 1991, 'Sliding toward nutrition malpractice, time to reconsider and redeploy', mimeo, Martin Forman Memorial Lecture, Hyatt Regency Hotel, Crystal City, June 24.

Binkin, N., Sullivan, K., Staehling, N., Nieburg, P., 1991, 'Rapid nutrition surveys: how many clusters are enough?' *Disasters*, 9 (2).

Borton, J., Shoham, J., 1985, 'Risk mapping and early warning: the Zambia case study', mimeo, Food and Agricultural Organisation, March 1985.

Borton, J., Shoham, J., 1989, 'A review of the Sudanese Red Crescent Society's Drought Monitoring Programme, Relief and Development Institute', A study commissioned by the Swedish Red Cross Society.

Briend, A., Dykewicz, C., Graven, K., Mazumder, R.N., Wojtyniak, B., Bennish, M., 1986, 'Usefulness of nutritional indices and classifications in predicting death of malnourished children', *BMJ*, 293: 373.

Briend, A., Zimicki, S., 1986, 'Validation of arm circumference as an indicator of risk of death in one to four year old children', *Nutrition Research*, 6: 249–261.

Briend, A., Wojtyniak, B., Rowland, M.G.M., 1987, 'Arm circumference and other factors in children at high risk of death in rural Bangladesh', *The Lancet*, 725–728.

Briend, A., Bari, A., 1989, 'Critical assessment of the use of growth monitoring for identifying high risk children in primary health care programmes', *BMJ*, 298: 1607.

Briend, A., Hasan, K.H., Aziz, K.M.M., Hoque, B.A., 1989a, 'Are diarrhoea control programmes likely to reduce childhood malnutrition? Observations from rural Bangladesh', *The Lancet*, 319–322.

Briend, A., Garenne, M., Maire, B., Fontaine, O., Dieng, K., 1989b, 'Nutritional status, age and survival: the muscle mass hypothesis', *European Journal of Clinical Nutrition*, 43: 715–726.

Briend, A., 1990, 'Is diarrhoea a major cause of malnutrition among the under-fives in developing countries? A review of available evidence', *European Journal of Clinical Nutrition*, 44: 611–628.

Briend, A., 1992, 'Etude des relations entre malnutrition et mortalité chez l'enfant au Senegal et au Bangladesh', PhD Thesis, University of Paris, France.

Brown, R.C., 1990, 'A simple system of nutrition surveillance for African communities', *Journal of Tropical Paediatrics*, 36: 162–164.

Buchanan-Smith, M., Mohammed Ibrahim Mohammed, 1991, 'Regional policy and food insecurity: the case of Darfur, Western Sudan', mimeo, Institute of Development Studies, Brighton, UK.

Buchanan-Smith, M., 1989, 'Evaluation of the Western Relief Operation 1987/1988', Ministry of Finance and Economic Planning, Khartoum, and the European Economic Community, Masdar Ltd, UK.

Buchanan-Smith, M., 1990, 'Food security planning in the wake of an emergency relief operation: The case of Darfur, Western Sudan', *IDS Discussion Paper*, No 278.

Buchanan-Smith, M., Davies, S., Lambert, R., 1991, 'A guide to famine early warning and food information systems in the Sahel and Horn of Africa – A review of the literature', *IDS Research Reports*, No 21.

Buckley, R., 1988, 'Food targeting in Darfur: Save the Children Fund's programme in 1986'. *Disasters*, 12 (2): 97–102.

Chambers, R., 1992, 'Rural appraisal: rapid, relaxed and participatory', IDS Discussion Paper, No 311.

Chandra, R.J., 1991, 'Nutrition and immunity: lessons from the past and new insights into the future', *American Journal for Clinical Nutrition*, 53: 1087–1101

Chen, L.C., Chowdhury, A.K.M., Huffman, S.L., 1980, 'Anthropometric assessment of energy-protein malnutrition and subsequent risk of mortality among pre-school aged children', *American Journal of Clinical Nutrition*, 33: 1836–1845.

Cogill, B., 1990, 'Information systems and the drought relief programme, Drought and the Rural Economy in Botswana an Evaluation of the Drought Programme 1982–1990', mimeo, Study Paper 4, prepared for Government of the Republic of Botswana.

Corbett, J., 1988, 'Famine and household coping strategies', *World Development*, 16 (9): 1092–1112.

Coulombier, D., Dionisius, J.P., Desve, G., 1991, 'Epi-nut Version 1.0: a software for analysis of nutrition surveys', Epicentre, 8 rue St. Sabin, 75011 Paris.

Currey, B., 1978, 'The famine syndrome: its definition for relief and rehabilitation in Bangladesh', *Ecology of Food and Nutrition*, 7: 87–98.

D'Souza, F., 1989, 'Famine and the art of early warning: the African experience', mimeo, report for ODA, SCF, London.

Davies, S., Buchanan-Smith, M., Lambert, R., 1991, 'Early warning in the Sahel and Horn of Africa: A review of the literature', Volume 1, IDS Research Report, No 20.

Dean, A.G., Dean, J.A., Burton, A.H., Dicker, R.C., 1990, 'Epi-info Version 5: a word processing, database, and statistics program for epidemiology on micro-computers'. USD, Inc, Stone Mountain, Georgia.

De Garine, I., Kappert, G., 1988, 'Coping with seasonal fluctuations in food supply among savanna populations: the Massa and Mussey of Chad and Cameroon', Ch 10: 210–259. In: *Coping with Uncertainty in Food Supply*, eds: Garine, I. de, Harrison, G.A., 1988, Clarendon Press, Oxford.

De Waal, A., 1988, 'Famine early warning systems and the use of socio-economic data', *Disasters*, Vol 12, No 1.

De Waal, A., 1989a, *Famine That Kills, Darfur, Sudan, 1984–1985*, Clarendon Press, Oxford.

De Waal, A., 1989b, 'Famine mortality: a case study of Darfur, Sudan 1984–5', *Population Studies*, 43: 5–24.

De Waal, A., 1989c, 'Population and health of Eritreans in Wad Sherifei: implications for the causes of excess mortality in famines', mimeo, Action Aid, London.

De Waal, A., 1993, 'War and famine in Africa', *IDS Bulletin*, 24 (4): 33–40.

Dibley, M.J., Goldsby, J.B., Staehling, N.W., Trowbridge, F.L., 1987a, 'Development of normalized curves for the international growth reference: historical and technical considerations', *American Journal of Clinical Nutrition*, 46: 736–748.

Dibley, M.J., Staehling, N., Nieburg, P., Trowbridge, F.L., 1987b, 'Interpretation of Z score anthropometric indicators derived from the international growth reference', *American Journal of Clinical Nutrition*, No 46: 749–62.

Dreze, J., Sen, A., 1989, *Hunger and Public Action*, Clarendon Press, Oxford.

Duffield, M., 1994, 'Complex political emergencies, with reference to Angola and Bosnia, An exploratory report for UNICEF', mimeo, School of Public Policy, University of Birmingham, UK.

Dugdale, A., Musgrave, A., Streathfield, K., Alsop-Shields, L., 1991, 'Diarrhoea and growth retardation', *Ecology of Food and Nutrition*, 25: 269–274.

Dyson, T., 1991a, 'On the demography of South Asian Famines, Part I', *Population Studies*, 45: 5–25.

Dyson, T., 1991b, 'On the demography of South Asian Famines, Part II', *Population Studies*, 45: 279–297.

Dyson, T., 1993, 'Demographic responses to famines in south Asia', *IDS Bulletin*, 24 (4): 17.

Fauveau, V., Briend, A., Chakraborty, J., Sarder, A.M., 1990, 'The contribution of severe malnutrition to child mortality in rural Bangladesh: implications for targeting nutritional interventions', *Food and Nutrition Bulletin*, 12 (3): 215.

Fleuret, A., 1986, 'Indigenous responses to drought in sub-Saharan Africa', *Disasters*, 10 (3): 224–227.

Frankenberger, F., Goldstein, D., 1990, 'Coping strategies of small farm households', *Association for Farming Systems Research Extension, Newsletter*, 1 (1).

Galvin, K., 1988, 'Nutritional Status as an indicator of impending food stress', *Disasters*, 12 (2): 147.

Gibb, C., 1986, 'A review of feeding programmes in refugee reception centres in Eastern Sudan, October 1985'. *Disasters*, 10 (1): 17–24.

Gomez, F., Galvan, R.R., Frenk, S., Cravioto Munoz, J., Chavez, R., Vazquez, J., 1956, 'Mortality in second and third degree undernutrition', *Journal of Tropical Paediatrics*, 2: 77–82.

Grandin, B.E., 1988, *Wealth Ranking in Smallholder Communities: A Field Manual*, Intermediate Technology Publications, London.

Habicht, J-P., Meyers, L.D., Brownie, C., 1982, 'Overview: indicators for identifying and counting the improperly nourished', *American Journal of Clinical Nutrition*, 35 (suppl): 1241–1254.

Heywood, P., 1982, 'The functional significance of undernutrition, growth and prospective risk of death in the highlands of Papua New Guinea', *Journal of Food and Nutrition*, 39, Part 1: 13–19.

Hill, A., 1987, 'Demographic responses to food shortages in the Sahel', Paper prepared for the FAO Expert Consultation on Population and Agricultural and Rural Development: institutions and policy, Rome, 29 June – 1 July, 1987.

Ibrahim, F.N., 1984, 'Ecological Imbalance in the Republic of Sudan – with Reference to Desertification in Darfur', Bayreuther Geowissenschafreiche Arbeiten, ed: Bayreuth Verlagsgesellschaft mbh.

Ibrahim, M.B., 1990, 'Drought, famine and disaster management in Darfur, Sudan', IFPRI, Famine and food policy discussion papers, Discussion Paper, No 4.

James, W.P.T., Ferro-Luzzi, A., Waterlow, J.C., 1988, 'Definition of chronic deficiency in adults, Report of a working party of the International Dietary Energy Consultative Group', *European Journal of Clinical Nutrition*, 42: 969–981.

Jaspars, S. and Young, H., (in preparation), 'Malnutrition and poverty in the early stages of famine – Findings in north Darfur, 1988–89'.

JNSP, 1989, 'The Joint WHO/UNICEF nutrition support programme in Iminga, Tanzania', 1983–1988 Evaluation Report, Dar es Salaam, Government of the United Republic of Tanzania, World Health Organization, United Nations Children's Fund.

Jodha, N.S., 1975, 'Famine and famine policies: some empirical evidence', *Economic and Political Weekly*, October 11.

Kasongo Project Team, 1983, 'Anthropometric Assessment of young children's nutritional status as an indicator of subsequent risk of dying', *Journal of Tropical Paediatrics*, 29, April: 69–75.

Katz, J., West, K.P., Tarwotjo, I. and Sommer, A., 1989, 'The importance of age in evaluating anthropometric indices for predicting mortality', *American Journal of Epidemiology* 130 (6): 1219.

Keen, D., 1991, 'A disaster for whom? Local interests and international donors during famine among the Dinka of Sudan', *Disasters*, 15 (2): 58–73.

Keen, D., 1992, *Refugees: Rationing the Right to Life. The crisis in emergency relief*: A Refugee Studies Programme Book, Zed Press, London.

Kelly, M., 1992, 'Entitlements, coping mechanisms and indicators of access to food: Wollo Region, Ethiopia, 1987–88', *Disasters*, 16 (4): 322–338.

Kielmann, A., McCord, C., 1978, 'Weight for age as an index of risk of death in children', *The Lancet*, 1: 1247.

Kloth, T.I., Burr, W.A., Davis, J.P., Epler, G., Kolff, C.A., Rosenberg, R.L., Staehling, N.W., Lane, J.M., Nichaman, M.Z., 1976, 'Sahel Nutrition survey', 1974, *American Journal of Epidemiology*, 103 (4): 383–390.

Koster, F.T., Curlin, G.C., Aziz, K.M.A., Azizal, H., 1981, 'Synergistic impact of measles and diarrhoea on nutrition and mortality in Bangladesh', *Bulletin of the World Health Organization*, 59: 901–908.

Lawrence, M., Yimer, T., O'Dea, J.K., 1994, 'Nutritional status and early warning of mortality in southern Ethiopia, 1988–1991', *European Journal of Clinical Nutrition*, 48: 38–45.

Lindskog, U., Lindskog, P., Carstensen, J., Larsson, Y., Gebre-Medhin, M., 1988, 'Childhood mortality in relation to nutritional status and water supply–a prospective study from rural Malawi', *Acta Paediatr Scand*, 77: 260.

Lindtjorn, 1990, 'Famine in southern Ethiopia 1985–86: population structure, nutritional state, and incidence of death among children', *BMJ*, 301: 1123–1127.

Longhurst, 1993, 'Integrating formal sample surveys and rapid rural appraisal techniques', Summary based on: Rapid Rural Appraisal Techniques and the Monitoring and Evaluation of IFAD Projects in Sudan, Centre for International Child Health, London.

Longhurst, R., Payne, P., 1981, 'Seasonal aspects of nutrition'. In: *Seasonal Dimensions to Rural Poverty*, eds: Chambers, R., Longhurst, R., Pacey, A., 1981, Pinter Publications, London.

145

Loutan, L., Lamotte, J-M., 1984, 'Seasonal variations in nutrition among a group of nomadic pastoralists in Niger', *The Lancet*, i: 945–947.

Lowgren, M., 1986, 'Nutrition surveillance as a tool for food aid response in LRC/RCS relief operation in Northern Darfur, Sudan', mimeo, League of Red Cross and Red Crescent Societies, Khartoum.

Mason, J., Habicht, J.P., Tabatabao, H., Valverde, V., 1984, Nutritional Surveillance, World Health Organization, Geneva.

Miller, D.C., Nichaman, M.Z., Lane, J.M., 1977, 'Simplified field assessment of nutritional status in early childhood: practical suggestions for developing countries', *World Health Organization Bulletin*, 55: 79–86.

Mitchell, J., Slim, H., Young, H., 1990, 'A review of Oxfam's current thinking and practice on food aid', mimeo, Oxfam, May.

Mollison, S., 1986, 'Socio-economic profiles in Darfur', mimeo, Save the Children Fund (UK), El Fasher.

Morgan, R., 1985, 'The development and applications of a drought early warning system in Botswana', *Disasters*, 9 (1): 44.

MSF, 1991, 'Assistance to populations in distress, Médecins Sans Frontières', Programme News, SCN News, No 7: 53.

Murray, M.J., Murray, A.B., Murray, N.J., Murray, M.B., 1975, 'Refeeding malaria and hyperferraemia', *The Lancet*, 653–4.

Murray, M.J., Murray, A.B., Murray, N.J., Murray, M.B., 1976, 'Somali food shelters in the Ogaden famine and their impact on health', *The Lancet*, 1283–1285.

Murray, M.J., Murray, A.B., 1977, 'Suppression of infection and its activation by refeeding – a paradox?' *Perspectives in Biology and Medicine*, 20: 471–483.

Nieburg, P., Berry, A., Steketee, R., Binkin, N., Dondero, T., Aziz, N., 1988, 'Limitations of anthropometry during acute food shortages: high mortality can mask refugees' deteriorating nutritional status', *Disasters*, 12 (3).

Ojaba, E., Abduljabbar A.F., 1992, 'Nutritional surveillance programme Oxfam Darfur', Evaluation Report, mimeo, Oxfam, Khartoum.

Pallister, D., 1994, 'When food relief comes out of the barrel of a gun', *The Guardian*, 7/5/94: 16.

Pearson, R., 1986, 'Lessons from Famine in Sudan, 1984–1986', mimeo, UNICEF, Khartoum.

Rahmato, D., 1988, 'Peasant survival strategies in Ethiopia', *Disasters*, Vol 12, No 4.

Reily, F., 1991, 'Drought responses of the Kabebish pastoralists in Northern Kordofan, Sudan: implications for famine early warning', mimeo, FAO.

Rivers, J.P.W., Holt, J.F.J., Seaman, J.A., Bowden, M.R., 1976, 'Lessons for epidemiology from the Ethiopian famines', *Annales de la Société Belge de Médecine Tropicale*, 56 (4/5): 345–356.

RRC, 1989, 'Nutritional Guidelines for Food Relief Rations', Relief and Rehabilitation Commission, Addis Ababa, Ethiopia.

Schofield, S., 1974, 'Seasonal factors affecting nutrition in different age groups and especially pre-school children', *Journal of Development Studies*, 11 (1): 22–40.

Scrimshaw, S.C.M., Hurtado, E., 1987, 'Rapid assessment procedures for nutrition and primary health care: Anthropological approaches to improving programme effectiveness', UNU/UNICEF and UCLA, Latin America Center.

Seaman, J., Holt, J., Rivers, J., 1978, 'The effects of drought on human nutrition in an Ethiopian Province', *International Journal of Epidemiology*, 7 (1): 31–40.

Sen, A., 1981, *Poverty and Famines, An Essay on Entitlement and Deprivation*, Clarendon Press, Oxford.

Shears, P., Berry, A.M., Murphy, R., Nabil, M.A., 1985, 'Epidemiological assessment of the health and nutrition of Ethiopian refugees in emergency camps in Sudan, 1985', *BMJ*, 295: 314–318.

146

Shears, P., 1991, 'Epidemiology and infection in famine and disasters', *Epidemiology and Infection*, 107: 241–251.

Shepherd, A., 1991, 'Improving food security at the household level; government aid and past drought development in Kordofan and the Red Sea Hills'. In: *To Cure All Hunger*, ed: Maxwell, S., IT Publications.

Shoham, J., 1987a, 'Does nutritional surveillance have a role to play in Early Warning of food crisis and in the management of relief operations', *Disasters*, 11: 282–285.

Shoham, J., 1987b, 'The role of project related nutritional surveillance in Early Warning: a case study of Catholic Relief Services in Ghana and Lesotho', mimeo, paper presented at a workshop on Experiences of Collection of and Use of Micro-level Data in Disaster Preparedness and Managing Emergency Operations.

Singer, H., Wood, J., Jennings, T., 1989, *Food aid, the challenge and the opportunity*, Oxford University Press.

Smedman, L., Sterky, G., Mellander, L., Wall, S., 1987, 'Anthropometry and subsequent mortality in groups of children aged 6–59 months in Guinea-Bissau', *American Journal of Clinical Nutrition*, 46: 369–373.

Sommer, A., Loewenstein, M.S., 1975, 'Nutritional status and mortality: a prospective validation of the QUAC stick', *American Journal of Clinical Nutrition*, 28: 287–292.

Spady, D.W., Payne, P.R., Picou, D., Waterlow, J.C., 1976, 'Energy balance during recovery from malnutrition', *American Journal of Clinical Nutrition*, 29: 1073–1078.

Stockton, N., 1986, 'Nutrition surveys', internal memorandum from field staff in south Sudan to Oxfam Head Office, Oxford, 10/11/86.

Sullivan, K.M., Gorstein, J., 1990, 'ANTHRO: software for calculating pediatric anthropometry. Version 1.01', Centers for Disease Control, Atlanta and World Health Organization, Geneva.

Swift, J., Gray, J., 1989, 'Report on Darfur Region food security policy and planning', mimeo, Report for the Overseas Development Administration.

Swift, J., 1989, 'Why are rural people vulnerable to famine?' *IDS Bulletin*, 20 (2).

Taylor, N., 1985, 'Report on Project Activities, March–May, 1985', Nutritional Surveillance and Drought Monitoring Project, mimeo, Oxfam, UNICEF and Darfur Regional Government, El Fasher.

Teklu, T., Von Braun, J., Zaki, E., 1991, 'Drought and famine relationship in Sudan: policy implications', International Food Policy Research Institute.

Teokul, W., Payne, P., Dugdale, A., 1986, 'Seasonal variations in nutritional status in rural areas of developing countries: a review of the literature', *Food and Nutrition Bulletin*, 8 (4): 7–10.

Thomas, M., Sharp, K., Maxwell, S., Hay, R., Jones, S., Low, A., Clay, E., Benson, C., 1989, 'Food aid to sub-Saharan Africa: a review of the literature', Occasional Papers, Number 13, World Food Programme, Rome.

Tomkins, A., 1986, 'Protein energy malnutrition and risk of infection', *Proceedings of the Nutrition Society*, 45: 289–304.

Tomkins, A., Watson, F., 1989, 'Malnutrition and infection: A review', ACC/SCN State of the Art Series, Nutrition Policy Discussion Paper, No 5.

Toole, M.J., Waldman, R.J., 1990, 'Prevention of excess mortality in refugee and displaced populations in developing countries', *Journal of the American Medical Association*, 263 (24): 3296–3302.

Trickett, V., 1993, 'Nutrition survey in Bardera, Somalia'. mimeo, International Rescue Committee, Bardera, Somalia, August 1993.

UNHCR, 1994a, 'Flash Appeal, 25 April – 31 May', 1994 Public Information Section, Geneva.

147

UNHCR, 1994b, 'UNHCR Update on Rwanda, 10 May 1994', Public Information Section, Geneva.

UNICEF, 1990, 'Strategy for improved nutrition of children and women in developing countries', A UNICEF Policy Review.

USAID, 1989, 'Nutrition in Times of Disaster', Report of an International Conference held at the World Health Organization Headquarters, Geneva, Sept 27–30, 1988, under the auspices of the UN ACC/SCN and the INFP, with partial support from USAID.

Waterlow, J.C., Buzina, R., Keller, W., Lane, J.M., Nichaman, M.Z., Tanner, J.M., 1977, 'The presentation and use of the height and weight data for comparing the nutritional status of groups of children under the age of 10 years', *Bulletin of the World Health Organization*, 55: 489–498.

Waterlow, J.C., Tomkins, A.M., 1992, 'Nutrition and infection', Ch 11. In: *Protein Energy Malnutrition*, by Waterlow, J.C., Edward Arnold.

Watts, M., 1988, 'Coping with the market: uncertainty and food security among Hausa peasants', Ch 11. In: *Coping with Uncertainty in the Food Supply*, eds: de Garine, I., Harrison, G.A.

WFP, 1991, Food Aid Review, World Food Programme, Rome.

Whitcombe, E., forthcoming, *Famine mortality*, Oxford University Press, Delhi.

WHO, 1976, 'Methodology of nutritional surveillance', Report of a Joint FAO/UNICEF/WHO Expert Committee, WHO Technical Report Series, No 593.

WHO, 1987, 'Global Nutritional Status, Anthropometric Indicators', Nutrition Unit, Division of Family Health, WHO, Geneva.

Williams, C., 1986, 'Report of March–April Survey 1986, Nutritional Surveillance and Drought Monitoring Project', mimeo, Oxfam, UNICEF and Darfur Regional Government, El Fasher.

Winer, N., Zins, J., 1984, 'An assessment of the nutritional status of children from 1–5 years of age in Kordofan Region', mimeo, Oxfam and UNICEF, Khartoum, 15 September, 1984.

Winer, N., 1985, 'Darfur Tour Report, 19 February', mimeo, Oxfam, Khartoum.

Yambi, O., Latham, M.C., Habicht, J.P., Haas, J.D., 1991, 'Nutrition status and the risk of mortality in children 6–36 months old in Tanzania', *Food and Nutrition Bulletin*, 13 (4): 271.

Young, H., 1992, *Food Scarcity and Famine, A Practical Guide to Assessment and Response*, Oxfam Practical Guide Series, Oxfam, Oxford.

Young, H., Jaspars, S., 1992, 'Nutritional surveillance; help or hindrance in times of famine?' Paper for discussion at a workshop at the Institute of Development Studies, 8/5/92, University of Sussex.

Young, H., Jaspars, S., 1995, *Malnutrition, disease and death in times of famine*, Disasters Journal, 19 (2).

INDEX

149